ONE BREATH,
THEN ANOTHER

a memoir

AMANDA ERIN MILLER

LUCID RIVER PRESS

For my mother, Terry Miller, my biggest fan

Contents

Counting Sheep   1

Cigarettes and Lettuce   8

Her Breath Smelled Like Chocolate   18

Mirror, Mirror on the Wall   25

Your Particular Smile   51

What is Language?   60

Home   81

Healer, Heal Thyself   86

Inside a Box Inside a Hole   91

What Now?   108

Eeeeendeeaahhh   116

No One Wears Shoes Here   123

Hari Om   146

Ninety to One Hundred Years   162

Vomen   170

Silence   175

Teaching   179

So Fucking Peaceful   182

Gratitude   190

Counting Sheep

When I opened my eyes, I was sitting on an old wicker chair, alone in a dark wood-paneled room. I was three years old, wearing my flannel "My Little Pony" nightgown with the pink ruffled sleeves. My short legs swung back and forth in midair. Two curly brown ponytails were mounted high on each side of my head.

I tried to get out of the chair, but I had been belted in tightly and could not find a buckle to release me. I searched frantically. It was dark and musty. How did I get there? Where were my parents? I listened hard for sound, some sign that a person might be in there with me. The overwhelming silence made my ears ache as they strained hard to hear something, anything.

Panic rose in my throat and I began to sob. I had to get out. I wanted to go home. I wanted my mom.

Suddenly, there were footsteps. I stopped crying and held my breath. There were two sets. Strong. Getting louder and louder. I clenched my jaw in fear.

"Is someone crying?" a male voice bellowed.

I released a whimper, unable to help myself.

"Yes, I believe someone is." Another male voice.

I bit the side of my hand to try to make the crying stop. The footsteps sped up until there was breath on the back of my neck. I stared at the ground as two sets of dirty black patent leather shoes appeared and stopped, pointing toward me. My gaze panned steadily up to two sets of black suit pants and black suit jackets, then two thick necks, and, finally, facial outlines hidden in thick shadow. I cried harder and dug my teeth deeper into my hand.

"You know what we do to little girls who cry?" one of the men over-enunciated, his lips winding around his words like snakes. He pulled a giant silver butcher knife out of his pocket, took a step toward me, and waved it below my nose. I shrieked and wiggled madly in my chair, unable to move.

The other man leaned down. "There's no use struggling," he moaned gruffly into my ear. This only made me scream louder. A dark red light poured over the men, but their faces remained shrouded in darkness. The one who had just spoken cupped his palms over my ears then pressed them hard, holding my head in place. The other man slunk behind me. In the pool of empty red light, I saw the shadow of the knife in the air. A wail barreled up and out from deep in my guts, nearly exploding my lungs and voice box. Then I felt a gag in my mouth, and my shrieks dissolved into gravelly moans. I stared at the knife's shadow, still raised above my head, my eyes wide with terror as I watched it come down. I felt it hack into the back of my skull. The pain was explosive, then drained into numbness. Both men laughed maniacally. I squeezed my eyes shut and braced myself as the knife struck again. Blood trickled down the back of my head and neck, cold and syrupy. I was getting dizzier. My eyes popped open to find the red light was brighter. The maniacal laughter was louder. Then the hands lifted off my ears, and I felt the sole of a shoe hard against my spine. I fell forward in slow motion. As I got closer to the ground, the pool of bright red light turned into thick blood.

Right as I was about to hit the ground, I was sweating violently in my bed, shaking and crying. I glanced up at the eerie shadows on my wall; one resembled a witch's head, one a goblin, and one a deranged rabid dog. Clutching my doll under my armpit, I scampered out of my room through the hall into my parents' room, leapt onto the king-sized bed, crawled toward my sleeping parents, and shimmied my small three-year old body between theirs, waking them. I turned toward my mom, crossed my arms over my chest and pressed myself into her back beneath the familiar cloud of frizzy red hair. She was the ultimate safety; she would protect me.

For several months, I had been having nightmares and running to sleep in my parents' bed. My mom welcomed me, but my father always tried to nudge me back to my room. I never left, and he usually just got tired and gave up. But he had been growing steadily more irritated by my middle-of-the-night appearances.

"Amanda, go back to your room," he muttered, his head against the pillow.

"No, I don't want to, I'm scared."

"There's nothing to be scared of," he said, sitting up and rubbing his eyes. "You're a big girl. Now show Daddy what a big girl you are and go back to bed."

"No, I want to stay with Mommy."

"Terry, make her go back to her room. This is your fault; you're enabling her." His tone was sharper, more impatient.

"What's the difference?" my mother sighed, half asleep.

"What's the difference? I've had it with this!" he yelled, standing, yanking his pants off the floor and pulling them up over his boxers.

"When I come back, I expect you to be in your own bed, do you understand?" he shouted in my face and stomped off.

His anger vibrated in my chest, stirring my own rage. He didn't understand, and he couldn't control me. I clenched my fists and bit my lower lip.

"David, where are you going?" called my mom.

"For a drive!" he screeched and slammed the bedroom door.

After a long pause, my rage deflated. I unclenched my fists and curled back up against my mom.

She took a breath and said, "You'd better go back to your room.

My mom turning against me was too much. Anger rushed back into my chest like a tub filling with water.

"But I don't want to. I want to stay here with you. I had a scary dream."

"I know, but it was just a dream, and you *are* a big girl. Big girls stay in their beds all night. Anyway, you think Daddy's mad now?

He's going to be really mad if you are here when he gets back, and we don't want that. Okay?"

"But I can't sleep."

"So count sheep."

"I want to stay here," I whined, tears rolling down my cheeks. I felt desperate. I couldn't believe she was kicking me out.

"I'm not kidding," she said, moving her body away from mine.

Anger rose from my chest to my throat.

"Fine!" I yelled, in the same tone as my father.

"Good, now give Mommy a kiss."

"No!" I screeched, just as my father had before leaving the room. Then, with doll in arm, I angrily stomped out and slammed the door, just as he had. But instead of going back to my room, I waited for him in the dark at the top of the stairs, my lungs heaving violently, heart pounding. I clenched my jaw hard. My bed was a dangerous place. I had to make him understand. I was going to win this.

It seemed like forever before he came back. Eventually I lay down at the top of the stairs and started dozing but woke myself up, committed to fighting sleep. Instead of counting sheep to relax me, I counted them to keep me awake. Each one jumped over a hurdle, wearing a different color bow around its neck. Eventually the bows turned into sweaters. Then the sheep became cows, then ponies, then horses. Finally, I got tired of counting animals, sat up, and began singing the *Sesame Street* theme song while picking at the carpet.

At last I heard the car pull up into the driveway and the front door slam. Keys clinked against the counter, footsteps scuttled across the floor. Then the light went on in the stairwell, and I had to squint because of the brightness. My father stared up at me from the bottom of the steps, and I stared back. I sat up straight, determined to make my case.

"What are you doing?" he bellowed through clenched teeth, his eyebrows contorted in anger. The energy of his anger penetrated my chest with such force that it nearly knocked me over. I hunched my shoulders, losing confidence.

"I just... I want to sleep next to Mommy," I whispered, scared. As he climbed the stairs and his face came into clearer focus, hazel eyes ablaze, I felt nervous. I had seen him mad before, but never this mad. Starting to think I was not going to win this after all, I hugged my doll to my chest. He hovered over me.

"You have your own bed and your own room for a reason!" he yelled. "You are too old for this!"

Gathering my courage, I stood up, puffed out my chest, and prepared to make my case. "But—"

His hand came down hard against my left cheek, taking me completely by surprise. My cheek burned, then throbbed. Stunned, I brought my hand to my face, looked up at him, and, after a long pause, erupted in tears. My parents had both given me light spankings from time to time for bad behavior, but no one had ever slapped me. I felt paralyzed, unsure of what to do with myself, or what to expect. I sat back down and buried my face in my arms.

Then there was a hand on my back, but this time the touch was soft and nurturing. I looked up to see my father kneeling beside me. All the anger had drained from his face.

"I'm sorry," he said softly. "Let's go downstairs." He held out his hand, the same one that had slapped me moments before.

I nodded in agreement, wiped my cheeks, reached for his hand, and gave my weight over as he hoisted me up to stand. We padded slowly down the stairs as my crying fizzled to a whimper.

When we reached the living room, he sat at the end of the couch and turned on the lamp. I plopped down across from him, the yellow lamplight enveloping his plump body. The red light from my dream flashed through my mind as our cat jumped up onto my lap, startling me. I shuddered, then began absentmindedly stroking her fur.

"I'm really very sorry for what I did," he said. "That wasn't right, and I will never do it again."

"Okay," I said, curling my shoulders toward each other, looking past him. My cheek still burned.

"But it really is time for you to sleep in your own bed. Do you understand?"

"But I have scary dreams," I said, shifting my gaze to the carpet and scooting away from him. The cat leapt to the floor and scurried off.

"I understand, but what you have to realize is that they are just dreams. They are not real; they can't hurt you. When you wake up, remember you are in your own bed and we are right across the hall. Anyway, I bet if you stay in your bed and show your dreams that you're not afraid, eventually they will go away."

I looked up at him.

"Are you sure?"

"Yes, I am actually. I used to have scary dreams, too. And that's what I did, and they went away."

I took a moment to consider it.

"Do you feel ready to go back to your bed?" he asked in a near whisper.

"I don't think so. I'm not really tired right now."

"Well, we can sit here for a few minutes until you feel tired."

"Okay."

To avoid going back to my room, I started picking at the couch. I wasn't convinced about this "willing away my nightmares" business. I remembered the knife, and my chest tightened.

My father stood, and I nervously lifted my head to see what he was doing. He walked over to the record player on the table across the room, lifted the top, and lowered the needle. Simon and Garfunkel's "Sounds of Silence" cooed out the speakers. He came back, wrapped his arms around me, and I hugged him, relaxing. He lifted me up and held me. My head rested against his shoulder as he swayed slowly from foot to foot with the music. My eyelids felt very heavy, so I let them close and my body went limp, dissolving inside the rhythm of my father's sway and the lulling harmonies.

The next morning, I woke up in my bed, my doll tucked under my arm, the morning light spilling through the cracks in the blinds. Miraculously, I had fewer nightmares after that and never slept in my parents' bed again. But on the occasion when I did have a nightmare, I would tiptoe into their room and tap my father gently on the shoulder. He would get out of bed, hold my hand, and walk me downstairs. Then he would turn on Simon and Garfunkel, hoist me up in his arms, and rock me gently until my eyes closed. From then on, whenever I heard Simon and Garfunkel, I could still feel my head on his shoulder.

Cigarettes and Lettuce

"We're here!" called my father as the door flew open and he darted into the living room, carrying an overstuffed floral suitcase in each hand. As I flicked off the television, my two-year-old brother, Austin, and my six-year-old sister, Tiffany, and me (nine at the time) eagerly popped up from the couch. Grandma Florence strode in behind my father, wearing a baggy light pink blouse, knee-length blue skirt, flesh-colored stockings, and white sneakers, her short curly red hair freshly cut and dyed. As we ran up to greet her, she smiled, wrinkles gathering in the corner of her eyes, pale sagging skin aglow under the ceiling light. Smelling like she had been rescued from an attic and then hosed down with perfume, she planted her wet lips on each of us as my father eagerly ushered everyone into the dining room.

He hoisted her suitcases onto the table, and we all huddled around as she unzipped it, displaying her bounty. Packs of frozen brisket, London broil, roast beef, and steak from her Long Island kosher butcher were nestled between her nightgowns and blouses, along with noodle kugel, sponge cakes, and devil dogs. She visited us in San Diego every year when I was young, always toting my father's favorite foods at his request. As he studied her gifts, his eyes beamed with childlike exhilaration; I never saw him so happy.

"You kids ready for some delicious brisket tomorrow night?" he asked, rubbing his hands together.

"Yeah!" we exclaimed, feeding off his energy.

The next night when I was in my room doing homework, I heard the Beatles' *Sergeant Pepper* album blasting through the wall and my father singing along. He loved sixties rock music and had an impressive vinyl collection. Music playing always signaled a good mood, a welcome treat, considering he was usually grumpy after work. I abandoned my math and scurried out to the kitchen to find him standing over the counter, soaking the brisket in its own gravy and adorning it with chopped carrots and onions.

"This is going to be great," he said to me, and smiled. "Go finish your homework. I'll call everyone when it's ready."

Not only was the meal delicious, there was a unique sense of lightness around the table. Neither of my parents usually had the interest or patience for elaborate cooking, as both were tired after working, my father as a contracting officer for the Department of Defense (no matter how many times he tried to explain it, we never quite understood what that meant), and my mom as a substitute English teacher and a Hebrew school teacher. Instead, they took turns preparing simple things like spaghetti, but more often than not they would heat up frozen food. Meals were often rushed and filled with the forced conversation of "How was your day?", "Fine, and yours?", and my parents bickering about bills while we devoured the meal quickly, then zipped off to finish our homework or watch television.

But when my grandma came, it was really like a holiday. My father's love for the brisket of his youth was contagious. We sat at the table much longer than normal, savoring every bite and relishing each other's company. After dinner, my grandma went to sleep while the rest of us piled into my parents' bed to watch *Looney Tunes* or *The Simpsons*. It was tradition. For the rest of the week, music, the smell of meat, and an air of cheer would fill the house. Then Grandma Florence left and life returned to normal: frozen foods, forced conversation, and my father's unpredictable moods.

My grandma had been shoveling her love into my father's stomach his entire life. Florence and her husband, Rabbi Irving Miller, adopted him as an infant, after their twelve-year-old son died of polio at summer camp. They believed that my father's biological parents were Polish Holocaust survivors (as his birth name was William Kowalski), too weak and/or poor to care for a son. My father was essentially a replacement child. Florence used food as a way of overcompensating to prove her love and to combat the pain of losing her biological son. In doing so, she inadvertently sentenced my father to life in a portly body. He was permanently scarred by never knowing who his real parents were and by the notion that he was a stand-in for somebody else.

His adopted parents showered him with love and attention, but he was always haunted by the belief that their love was really intended for their dead son. He wanted someone to love him for him and struggled with self-esteem issues his whole life, an estranged free-floater in the world. Despite the assumptions about his biological parents' situation, he couldn't help but feel abandoned and wonder why they didn't love him enough to keep him. Food became his drug of choice, his method for smothering all the unresolved feelings. In his early teens, he complimented his food addiction with a nicotine addiction, and, forever after, the two accompanied him on his way.

Since he spent the majority of his life overweight, his cholesterol levels were always of concern, and early in his thirties he developed the heart condition arteriosclerosis (hardening of the arteries), eerily, the same condition his adopted father had. Still, the diagnosis did not inhibit his eating patterns. Even a heart condition could not keep him away from his beloved brisket. However, the artery in his left leg eventually became so clogged that he started dragging the leg around like dead weight; he walked very slowly. The carotid artery in the left side of his neck accumulated such a severe blockage that his pulse could no longer be detected on that side. As time went by, his cholesterol levels rose steadily, and his cardiologist ultimately told him that if he didn't lose weight, he would undoubtedly suffer a heart attack.

That night, unaware of his doctor visit, my mom had prepared spaghetti and meatballs, a meal high on my father's love list. "Dinner!" she called out in her customary manner as my brother, sister and I came running. We were already scarfing down the meal when my mother hollered to my father, louder this time, "Honey! Dinner!" It was most unlike him to dawdle on his way to the table. Moments later, he ambled through the doorway, hanging his head, walked to the refrigerator, and pulled out a full head of romaine lettuce. He plopped down at the table, dumped the lettuce on his plate, and began peeling off the leaves and shoving them into his mouth.

"Honey, are you okay?" she asked.

He didn't speak or look up from his plate. He devoured over half the head of lettuce before getting up, tossing it into the fridge like a football, and trudging back to his and my mom's bedroom, leaving the rest of us sitting at the table, mouths agape. My mom got up to follow him while the rest of us picked at the remnants of our meal. Once Austin finished the food on his plate, he reached over to Tiffany's, grabbed a handful of spaghetti drenched in sauce, and shoved it in his mouth, the sauce leaking down his chin onto his shirt. "Gross," said Tiffany, patting him lightly on the shoulder. We both laughed. I pushed my leftovers toward him, and he did it again. We shook our heads; two-year-olds were hilarious.

Minutes later, my mom returned and said, "Today the doctor told Daddy that he needs to be on a strict diet." She looked stressed and didn't even notice that my brother was covered in noodles and sauce. My sister and I shrugged, dumped our plates in the sink, and ran to the living room to fight over the remote control, our brother toddling after us. We didn't fully understand what she was telling us and didn't believe it anyway. Our father had announced he was going on a diet several times, usually at the end of a big meal. We just assumed that night he was in one of his typical bad moods.

But with the threat of a heart attack, he really had resolved to follow a strict diet, so strict it turned into a "Fuck You, Self" weight-loss plan. He subsisted on coffee, cigarettes, caffeine pills, diet pills, Diet Coke, a handful of saltines for a midmorning snack, half of a milkshake for lunch (his one indulgence), and lettuce. Once, when I came into the kitchen for water in the middle of the night, I found him standing in the walk-in pantry in the dark, chomping saltines with intense desperation, crumbs falling from his hands to the floor. It took a moment for him to notice me, and when he did, he stopped mid-bite and froze, like a stunned rat. I didn't say anything, just poured my water and went back to my room, trying to strike the disturbing image from my mind.

Meanwhile, he was steadily increasing his smoking habit and developed such a severe hacking cough that it often woke me up at night. He never smoked in the house but smoked in the car with the window down while driving my brother, sister, and me to school. I hated the smell and how it made him cough.

Once Tiffany found his carton of Doral cigarettes in the cabinet and threw them away. That night as we were getting ready for bed, we heard my father scream as loud as he could, "Everyone get in here!" We came running to see what the matter was. He was standing in the kitchen in his bathrobe and slippers, eyes bulging, a long blue vein protruding from the center of his forehead.

"Do you think it's a funny joke to hide Daddy's cigarettes?" he shouted. "Tell me...now!"

Tiffany walked over to the cabinet under the sink, opened the door, and brought out the plastic wastebasket, displaying the carton on top. She didn't do a very good job of hiding it. My father scampered over, scooped it up, placed his hand on her shoulder, and looked her in the eye. His face relaxed, and he took a breath and said softly, "Promise me you won't do that again." She nodded. He looked up at the rest of us and, in an even softer voice, said "Good night." He lifted his hand off her shoulder and went out the front door. Through the window, we watched him light a cigarette, take a drag, cough, and spit.

"Well, it's bedtime," said my Mom. "Let's go. I'll tuck you in."

As I lay in bed after she left the room, I thought about how mean he had just been, and I knew it was because he was starving.

I thought about how cranky I got if I missed a meal, and was unable to imagine how I would feel if I were eating like he was. I wished he would eat better so he could be nice again; I missed him.

My father wasn't sleeping much in general because he was so hungry and hyper-caffeinated. He started waking up at 3:30 every morning, making him very irritable by the end of the day. Ultimately, he managed to lose eighty pounds in a single year. By the end of the year, he looked decades older. His face was gaunt, loose skin sagging where his full cheeks had once been. His dark brown hair was mostly gray, and his skin took on a sickly yellowish hue. His collarbones protruded like freshly unearthed fossils. He was drowning inside his clothes and looked ill.

Once, when he came to pick me up from school, as he was walking toward me from the car, my friend asked, "Why does your grandpa pick you up from school? Where are your parents?" I was embarrassed. "That's actually my dad," I said. In public, more people started making this mistake.

As the weight drained out of him, so did all sense of joy. He really had become the walking dead, a miserable form devoid of spirit. When he wasn't at the office, he was camped out in his room in front of the television with the door closed. Whenever he emerged, he barreled through the house like a storm cloud.

One evening, he staggered into the kitchen, spewing mucous into a handkerchief, reeking of cigarettes, looking especially pale. My mom was boiling water for macaroni, my sister and I were sitting at the table doing our homework, and my brother was on the carpet pushing toy trucks. My father poured himself a glass of water and chugged it down, then went to the sink to wash it, only to discover there was no dishwashing liquid. He swiveled toward my mother and erupted.

"Where is your head? How could you forget the soap? We discussed it this morning! What is the matter with you?"

"I'm sorry, honey, I'll go get it now if that would make you feel better," she humored him.

"No, don't get it now!" he barked, pounding his fist against the counter. "It's your night to make dinner for the kids! I made it last night. Do I really have to do everything around here? We'll just let the dishes sit tonight. You can get it tomorrow."

He returned the bottle of water to the refrigerator and then proceeded to reprimand my brother for leaving his toys out in the living room and my sister for not putting food back into the cupboard. "You're all lazy, thoughtless, careless, and spoiled!" he shouted at us. I stood at the counter, emptied the last ice cube into my glass, set the ice tray down, and returned to the dining room table, where I had been reading.

"Fill that back up and put it in the freezer!" he screamed at me.

The force of his voice blasted through me, evoking the early memory of his hand crashing across the side of my face. I winced as blood rushed to my cheek and electricity surged down my fingers.

"I'll do it later," I said coldly, focusing intently on the tabletop.

"No, you won't. Later you'll forget. Do it now," he commanded.

My cheeks were burning, thoughts crashing into each other like freight trains into brick walls. His temper was fiercely provoking mine. I felt like I was being attacked from the inside and out.

"I'll do it later!" I screamed back at him with such force that it surprised me.

My lungs were heaving. I bit my lip. Even though I wasn't looking at him, I could feel the thick, tense energy between us. Everyone else had stopped what they were doing, waiting to see what was going to happen. I held my breath.

My father took a step toward me, then abruptly turned toward the hallway, dragging his leg back to his bedroom, emitting heavy chest coughs along the way. I exhaled deeply. However, the storm had not passed. At the dinner table that night, when he realized my mom had forgotten to buy lettuce, he flew into such a rage that he chucked a glass plate at the wall.

We all froze in shock, my father included. He had surprised himself. His eyes turned pink and puffy; he looked like he was on the verge of tears. "I'm sorry," he said, and stood up quickly, pushed in his chair, and scurried down the hallway. We heard the door slam shut as my mom grabbed the broom and dustpan out of the pantry, swept up the glass, and sat down. We finished the rest of our meal in silence.

I wanted to do something to make him feel better, to hug him and tell him I loved him, but he often made me too scared to be able to talk to him, let alone come near. It was as if he were walking around wearing electric armor; if I came too close, I might get shocked.

My mom never talked to us about what was going on with our father. We all just tried to be on our best behavior when he was around. He spent most of his time locked in his room anyway, so it was just in the short moments he appeared that the air would grow thick and tense and we would brace ourselves for his potential detonation. Sometimes he exploded, sometimes merely passed through. Then we exhaled and moved on with our days.

After a doctor's visit to evaluate his progress, he was reprimanded for causing even more harm to his body. The increase in his smoking had caused such severe scarring of his lung tissue that he was running a serious risk of emphysema. His body required a certain number of calories a day to function properly, and he was eating well under that requirement. The doctor suggested he see a nutritionist to help him work out an appropriate diet plan and to quit smoking, but he did neither. He increased his food intake, but only consumed foods that were diet, fat-free, and sugar-free. He was never able to enjoy food the way he had before yet remained obsessed with it, spending an eternity in the supermarket, reading labels and considering various diet products. He spent hours on the weekends at the kitchen table, sipping coffee, eating fat-free, sugar-free chocolate pudding, and cutting out coupons.

My dad never ate the meals my mom prepared. Instead he came to the table with that box of saltines, a pack of diet salami, and his head of lettuce. Only once did she comment on how what he was doing was rude.

"Hey, worry about yourself. Leave me alone," he retorted snidely.

She never commented on any of his behavior again, at least not in front of us, so we didn't, either. He was too obsessed with himself to take much of an interest in our lives. And the majority of the interactions we did have continued to be negative, usually him criticizing us in some way.

As a result, my mom became the safe, reliable, loving parent, the one actually involved in our lives. She inquired about school with genuine interest, asked us about and helped us with homework. We went to her when we were upset or had a problem.

In spite of how he criticized her, my father really did admire my mom. One morning, while he was driving Tiffany and me to school and Austin to daycare, he blew smoke out the window and said, "Your mother really is the most selfless person I know." He was saying it more to himself than to us. It seemed to be a sudden revelation that parenting required selflessness, like it just dawned on him that a relationship with his children would take effort.

"You guys know I love you," he said suddenly.

"We love you, too, Daddy," we said, our voices overlapping.

With slightly more food in his system resulting in slightly more energy, he resolved to make a greater effort. One Sunday morning, I woke to the Fleetwood Mac record *Rumours* blasting in the living room and the sound of my father singing along. It had been so long since he'd played any music. I tumbled out of bed to see what was happening. He was dancing around, smiling and singing. Austin and Tiffany soon hobbled in curiously, rubbing their sleepy eyes. The sight of my father in a joyous state was surreal and infectious. We joined in the dancing, the three of us grabbing hands and spinning in circles until we fell to the floor laughing, like we were celebrating his recovery.

"You kids want to go to the park for a baseball catch?"

"Sure!"

We went to the park and spent a couple of hours fielding pop flies and grounders, then came home, made lemonade, and watched a Cleveland Indians game together on the couch. He really loved baseball, and the Indians were his favorite team. His sister was eighteen years older than he and married a man from Cleveland when he was three. As a child, my father decided he was going to root for all Cleveland teams. He stuck to it for the rest of his life.

We thought something might be changing. Maybe his spirit really was improving. We were wrong. The next day, he screamed at us that we were going to be late for school. Why were we so lazy, we had to hurry up, he had to get to work. That night, he locked himself right back in his room, came out when my mom called him for dinner, brought out his own cold meal, ate it quickly without out a word, then left the table to go back to his room. Still, the part of him that wanted to enjoy life continued to fight against the part that hated himself. Periodically, he poked his head out of his hole like a star piercing black sky.

Her Breath Smelled Like Chocolate

"I know you don't believe me now," my mother said, "but you really will have a wonderful time. You just have to trust me."

I cried and pounded the floor, the bed, the walls, then plopped down, shoulders heaving, screaming until I was hoarse. She watched me, standing with her arms crossed over her chest, unimpressed. Eventually I had exhausted myself to the point where I could no longer move or produce sound.

"Are you done?" she asked.

I stared at the wall, refusing to answer or move. It was the summer before sixth grade, and my mom had gotten a job teaching drama at the Jewish sleep-away camp, Camp Ramah in Ojai, California, just south of Santa Barbara. As a trade, the camp was letting her children go for free. Both my parents had attended sleep-away camp as kids and were still nostalgic for it. They had always wanted to send us but had been restricted by finances. With my mom's new job, we could go. I had no interest in camp and was livid that they were deciding how I would spend my summer.

Exhausted, I crawled toward my bed, stood up, and slid between the sheets. My mother pulled the covers over me, kissed me good night, turned off the light, and left the room. I rolled over, my heart in knots. Six weeks. I was going to camp whether I liked it or not.

The next morning, my father drove us to the University of Judaism in Los Angeles to catch the staff bus to camp. He would be staying home by himself for the summer. Despite the fact that he was always voluntarily isolating himself, I worried about him being completely alone for so long. Then I let the thought slide as I became consumed by my own problems. Why did I have to go? I gave him a weak hug goodbye, climbed the steps of the bus angrily, walked to the back, and found a seat by the window, as far away from my mom as possible. The bus pulled out of the parking lot, onto the freeway, and drove me into the unknown.

Two hours later, we rolled down a narrow road bordering orange and avocado groves and pulled into camp. I got out of the bus and stepped onto the concrete at the base of a wide tree-lined green field surrounded by cabins. Big beautiful hills encompassed camp beneath a dome of sunny blue sky. The grounds were immaculate and seemed to sparkle. Though I was still nervous to be there, I was intrigued, having never before seen such a place.

"What do you think?" my mom asked me, laying her hand on my shoulder. I squirmed out from under it, determined to be miserable until there was a real reason to be otherwise. We got our bags and lugged them to her staff room across the way. Then we deposited my four-year-old brother into the preschool group with the other young staff children, and my mom walked my sister and me to the center hill to find our counselors and bunkmates.

The first day of camp was a sight to behold. All the counselors stood with big welcome signs, singing and clapping as the buses pulled in. I felt shy and nervous watching the commotion, wishing I could disappear. Kids ran out of the buses, reuniting with friends with such fierce hugs that some of them actually toppled over onto the grass. It was loud and chaotic, kids running frantically up the hill to see what bunk they were in and who their counselors were. I thought about my dad at home in front of the television and how I wished I were sitting beside him. I wasn't convinced I had the kind of pep necessary for this place.

"Remember I'm here, but only come to me if it's an absolute emergency. I love you," my mom said, kissing us each on the cheek. She turned to go to her room, and I watched her back get smaller and smaller then disappear behind a building. Unlike me, my sister was excited and ran confidently into the clump of bouncing bodies. I made my way over apprehensively, wincing as faces came into view. My counselors greeted me with a disarming amount of cheer. They gave me a name tag and introduced the other girls in my bunk, who were so bubbly and smiley I wanted to spray them with a hose. It wasn't that I was opposed to happiness; this just seemed over the top. I bit my lip as I shook everyone's hand.

Once all sixteen girls had arrived, our four counselors walked us up the hill to our bunk. We played an icebreaker game with M&Ms where each color had a different question attached to it, from "What's your favorite ice cream flavor?" to "What's your biggest fear?" I found it cheesy and awkward, and continued to crave my couch and my television.

The first few days were painfully long. We woke up early to eat and go to services, and then the rest of the day was filled with activities like sports, bunk bonding, and swimming. Most of the girls wore bright stylish two-piece suits to the pool. I, however, having been on the YMCA swim team for the past two years, sported my black Speedo racing suit and was extremely self-conscious about it. While the girls all hung out in the shallow end, splashing around and chatting, I swam laps in the one lane that was set up. When pool time was over and they continued their conversations on the way back to our bunk, I lingered behind, feeling hollow.

After breakfast on the third day, we had to pick an elective among drama, art, jewelry making, basketball, or fencing. We sat on the grass in the middle of the hill while the elective leaders gave their pitches. The fencing teacher stood in full uniform, white suit and mask, and demonstrated some moves with his foil, which looked awfully cool. I felt my first flicker of excitement, picking fencing because I really wanted to wear that suit and swing that foil around. The group consisted of a bunch of nerdy, awkward boys and me. We followed the leader to the fencing room and suited up. The suit was hot, the helmet big and clunky, wobbling out of place every time I moved my head. I couldn't see very well out of the metal grid in front of my face.

Everyone sat in a clump, watching two people in a practice match while the teacher gave instructions. The boy with whom I had my match wasn't listening to any of the instructions. He kept stepping on my toes and poking that foil all over my body. I brought my arms up over my face to defend myself and eventually dropped my foil, but the kid persisted. The teacher called out, "Okay, enough!" But the kid seemed possessed and continued attacking me. Once I fell over, he eased up and took off his helmet, standing there and looking very pleased with himself. The teacher told everyone this was an example of what not to do, then knelt down and asked me if I was okay. "Yes," I said, trying to brush it off. "Are you sure?" he persisted as I stood up, losing my balance, growing more embarrassed. The boys giggled. "Yes," I repeated, wishing to melt into the floor. I pulled off my helmet and went to sit behind the group as the next couple got up. For the rest of the hour, I sat in shame, shoulders hunched, staring at my lap. It was going to be a long summer.

Later that afternoon, I got a letter from my dad. He said he was hanging in there at home by himself, but it was taking a while to get used to the quiet. He told me he really loved camp as a kid and believed I would grow to love it, too; I just had to give it some time. He included a newspaper clipping of the Indians baseball stats folded up inside the letter. I couldn't have cared less about how the Indians were doing that season, but still thought it was sweet that he included it, making me miss him even more. I wanted to go home and have a baseball catch with him, make lemonade, and watch a game.

Every night at bedtime, our counselors did a closing activity that included reading a story or poem, or singing a song. That night they read us a story about friendship from *Chicken Soup for the Soul*. The story made me feel even lonelier. After our counselors turned out the light, said good night, and left the bunk, most of the girls congregated on each other's beds, chatting and busting out secret candy and potato chip stashes to share, a nightly ritual. I rolled onto my side, hugged my pillow to my chest, and squeezed my eyes shut, feigning sleep, wishing to be part of the group. I wanted to go home to my dad. He could yell at me, reprimand me for a million things. I didn't care; I would take it. At least it was familiar. Not like this.

Tears leaked down my face, and I started sobbing quietly. I tried to muffle the sound by pressing the pillow over my mouth so none of the giggling girls would hear me cry. I felt stupid and wished I could disappear.

"Are you okay?" I heard a voice ask me from the edge of my bed.

I rolled over and saw the girl standing there. The yellow porch light outside my window illuminated her pale skin, short brown hair, and blue eyes. Her name was Celia. She slept in the bunk bed across from me. Until then, we had only exchanged polite smiles.

"Yeah, I'm fine," I said, wiping my eyes.

"Do you want to talk about anything?" she asked.

"I don't know," I said, sitting up. I was grateful for her noticing and seeming interested in me, but still wasn't quite sure how to engage with her. "Uh...okay," I finally said.

She climbed up the metal ladder to my bed and sat down.

"What's going on?" she asked.

"I'm not sure I really fit in here," I said, hugging my knees to my chest.

"Do you feel homesick?"

"I don't know...sorta...I guess."

She scooted toward me, leaned her chest in toward mine, and wrapped her arms around me. My friends at school had never hugged me before. Come to think of it, this was my first hug from a non-family member. At first I felt tense and nervous, my arms hovering above her back, and then I slowly relaxed and let my palms rest against her T-shirt. My nose was in her hair, which smelled like raspberry shampoo. Her breath smelled like chocolate. After about a minute, I stopped crying and pulled away.

"Do you want some Crunch bar?" she asked, pulling the chocolate out of her sweatshirt pocket.

"Okay."

We sat up for a long time, eating chocolate and talking about our families and how we were both nervous for middle school. I laughed at something while I had chocolate in my mouth, and it dribbled down my chin. She laughed at me. This made me laugh harder and spit up more chocolate, which sent us both into a giggle fit to the point where I had tears in my eyes and nearly peed the bed. Eventually we calmed down and decided we were both tired enough to sleep. Celia hugged me once more before climbing down the ladder and heading back to her own bed. I rolled over as the sound of crickets mingled with the sound of rustling leaves, lulling me into a warm, relaxed sleep.

After that, I felt a definite shift. No one was actually threatening or intimidating; I had just closed myself off. Once I opened up, I started to have a surprising amount of fun, able to be sillier and freer than I ever knew possible. We made up ridiculous dances for bunk activities, went on hikes, lay out on towels as our counselors strummed guitar under the stars. I started to see my counselors as being cool and wise, looking up to them and striving to emulate them. After a few more sessions, I got better at fencing and actually became quite good at it, really showing those boys up. We sang Hebrew songs in the dining hall after meals with all the energy we could muster and danced around the tables, so alive. At outdoor services every Friday night, with the sun setting, sky fading from blue to periwinkle, surrounded by mountains, everyone joined together and harmonized the prayers with their full voices, singing from their guts. I had been going to temple since I was a toddler and hated services. But camp services were different. There was an infectious spirit in the air. I reveled in the feeling of being part of this community, fully accepted, at peace with myself and my surroundings.

On the last night of camp, we had Banquet. This consisted of a big dinner, an extra-long song and dance session, and a slide show from the summer. Each bunk dressed up with a different theme. My bunk's theme was "Backwards," so we wore all our clothes backwards and thought it was the best idea ever. Boys asked girls to be their dates to Banquet, which involved holding hands while walking down the hill to the dining hall and sitting next to each other during the slide show after dinner. A boy named Ben asked me. He had blue eyes, lots of freckles, and straight long-ish light brown hair parted down the middle. We held hands and touched shoulders while watching the slide show. Then, after Banquet under a tree on the hill, he kissed me. It was my first kiss. His lips were soft. I felt a flutter in my chest, said good night, and ran back to my bunk to squeal to my friends. Several of them had their first kisses that night as well. We stayed up all night with our counselors, eating candy and chips, drinking soda, and reminiscing about the past weeks.

On the last morning of camp, everyone gathered in the dining hall after breakfast, waiting apprehensively for the buses to be called. Most kids were crying hysterically, hugging their friends like the world was ending. When the San Diego bus was announced, I felt like my insides were being ripped out of me. I squeezed everyone in my bunk to me one at a time, saving Celia for last. Tears and snot gushed out of me onto her shoulder. I joined my mom, brother, and sister outside. As the bus pulled me past the orange groves at the entrance, I experienced a sinking sensation of loss within my chest like never before, the gray sky casting dusty light on the trees outside my window.

Mirror, Mirror on the Wall

Camp introduced me to human connection on a level I had never known, implanting a permanent craving to connect the deepest part of me with the deepest part of others. I kept in touch with my camp friends through letters and phone calls for the first couple of months after the session ended. But then as we were all consumed by our home lives, we gradually lost touch, and I had to face my reality: middle school.

Everyone in sixth grade seemed equally disturbed by the new school circumstances, so people were looking to link up. I met some girls in my classes who became my crew, who introduced me to grunge bands like Nirvana and Hole. I enjoyed trying on grunge as an identity, shopping at thrift stores and wearing tattered baggy clothing and my first pair of Converse All Stars. It felt cool to be part of a scene for the first time, but the friendships were pretty superficial, nothing like camp. Nevertheless, socializing became an important part of my life, as I began talking on the phone regularly and hanging out with people outside our houses without parents around. It made me feel older and more independent. Still, I was supremely grateful when June rolled around and I could return to the hills and trees beneath that sparkling sunny sky.

Seventh grade began with the familiar post-camp depression. I sought my more superficial school friends to fill the void.

One morning between first and second period, I saw my friend Cora at her locker and approached her.

"Hey, what's up?" I asked.

"Not much," she said, continuing to look for something, her straight black hair falling over her face.

I didn't like that she wasn't looking at me. Something felt off.

"What are you doing after school today? Want to go down to the beach?" I asked, pretending not to notice.

"Uh, I would, but I'm going to the mall with Rachel," she said, dumping a book into the backpack she was balancing on her bent knee and tucking her hair behind her ear.

Rachel was one of the most popular girls at school.

"Okay, that's cool. What about tomorrow, then?"

"Look, I'm busy all week," she said, closing her locker.

"Okay..."

"Anyway, I gotta go. See you later," she said and sped off.

It wasn't just her. It seemed that all my friends had been reincarnated as bitches over the summer. The girls were all wearing makeup and tighter clothing, manifesting some arbitrary concept of "cool," while I was still sporting big baggy shirts and pants. Our group didn't eat together at lunch anymore; social climbing became everyone's new obsession. I tried to eat with old friends in new formations with some of the popular girls, but I was largely ignored and felt uncomfortable, so I gradually took to sitting by myself at lunch, lacking the energy or drive to make myself seen or heard by people who had little interest in me. People started to drink, smoke pot, and make out in the hallways. My confidence drained, and I lost all sense of comfort within my skin. At lunch, while everyone else around me was eating and chatting, I wrote in my journal, a spiral notebook covered in masking tape and painted black, which I had begun scribbling in compulsively.

Mirror, mirror on the wall
Who's the most hideous of them all
Whose horrifying face can draw a gasp
Out of all eyes upon which it grasps?
When the possessor dies out,
The world surely will shout,
Maggots will feast, ground will be fertile.
Mirrors won't shatter, blood won't curdle.

The rest of the year I retreated deeper into myself, becoming an isolated loner. By the time summer rolled around, I felt different, more protected, not as free. Then at camp I met Nina. She wore slips, thick black eyeliner, Doc Martens laced up to her knee, and she carried a tin Strawberry Shortcake lunchbox as a purse. She was pale with blue eyes and long, straight blonde hair. Nina didn't seem to care at all what others thought of her. I wanted to be like that. One day during free time, as I was walking from my tent down the hill with Sylvia Plath's *Ariel* under my arm, I saw her sitting alone under a tree, reading a book. I sat down next to her.

"What are you reading?" I asked.

"*Foxfire* by Joyce Carol Oates," she said, looking up at me, bangs in her eyes. Her lips stretched into a closed-mouth half smile.

"Cool, what's that about?" I asked, studying her studded cat collar and black negligee.

"It's about this all-girl gang. Pretty awesome." I wanted to be her friend right away. "What kind of stuff do you read?" she asked.

"Lately it's been mostly poetry," I said, showing her my book.

"Oh, Sylvia Plath. Intense and amazing." She lowered her gaze to the ground and began to pick at the grass. I felt an immediate connection to her; we were both melancholic and brooding. I started picking at the grass as well.

"Where do you go to school?" I asked.

"The San Diego Jewish Academy, but I'm going to Muirlands next year."

"That's where I go. I hate it."

"I hate my school, too. But I thought public school might be a little better."

"I'm Amanda," I said.

"Nina."

For the rest of the four-week session, we were nearly inseparable. I was excited that she would be coming to my school: I finally had a cohort. Once the school year began, I spent most of my free time at her house, where she introduced me to Tori Amos and Marilyn Manson. I dyed my brown hair black and donned black makeup, dog collars, and fishnet stockings. I found this new identity suitable; it was a way to artfully express what was going on inside me.

Nina and I wrote notes to each other every day at school, complete with drawings, poems, and song lyrics. We passed them to each other in class or in the hallways or sometimes left them as surprises in each other's lockers. We spent our weekends shopping in thrift stores and stealing makeup and jewelry from drugstores. We stayed up late at her house, talking, baking brownies, listening to music, making collages, and photographing each other in our most creative thrift store–inspired costumes. I reveled in her company, my first best friend. We were different from all the other annoying people in middle school. Together, in our rebellious melancholic bubble, we were invincible.

"I woke up this morning feeling like shit," I said to Nina one day at lunch. We were sitting together in the corner of the courtyard. I wore a tight black shirt, fluffy red petticoat, black fishnets, maroon Doc Martens, five necklaces, one of which was a wallet chain, thick black eyeliner, and black lipstick. Nina wore a long white slip with lace at the bottom, blue and white striped socks up to her knee, black steel-toed boots, vamp red lipstick, a cat collar, and a tan trench coat. Her hair was streaked with blue and purple; I had dyed it for her a few weekends before. "I begged my parents to let me stay home," I said, "but of course they wouldn't let me. God, I hate them."

She stared at me blankly, like she was high, and bit into her cheese sandwich.

Then this pretty popular girl Alexis approached, wearing tight jeans and a low-cut black shirt. She had developed early and already had cleavage. I glanced down at my flat chest, wondering what the hell Alexis was doing near us.

"Hey, Nina, you still coming over later today?"

"Yeah," she said.

"Cool, see you then," Alexis said and walked off, ignoring me entirely.

"You're friends with her?" I asked, astounded.

"Yeah, whatever," she said with the same flat affect. "I cut myself again last night," she said, rolling up the sleeves of her trench coat, displaying deep red slashes. I stared at them resentfully, unsure as to how she wanted me to respond. "I cried all night. My mom took me to the psychiatrist this morning. So now I'm on this new anti-depressant, Zoloft," she stated matter-of-factly, sipping her Diet Coke. Lately she had been acting weirdly distant and was making everything about her. I took her slashed wrists as a challenge. How deep was *my* pain? Could it compare to hers? What lengths would *I* be willing to go to express it?

There was a proud sexiness to her sadness, but mine didn't quite fit me that way. I wore it like a frumpy dress, ugly and awkward. The popular crowd, both boys and girls, slowly grew enamored with Nina, finding her dark and intriguing. I felt invisible.

Nina gradually became more and more narcissistic, absorbing herself deeply into her own pain and the attention it elicited. I was always there for her when she needed to talk, but she never for me. As she racked up more friends and our relationship grew increasingly strained, we spoke less and less and ultimately drifted apart. When we finally stopped talking, I continued to wear outlandish clothing, listen to the same music, read and wrote poetry, but it all felt empty without a partner.

People averted their eyes from me in the hallways. My science teacher made fun of my black and white striped tights in front of the class. One time, the surfer boys threw food at me during lunch. "Freak!" they called out and laughed. How come Nina could dress like that and be cool but if I dressed like that I was a freak? I ran to the bathroom, cried, and wrote pained poetry. I read Sylvia Plath and identified with her, convinced I was the saddest, loneliest person on earth.

The more alienated I became, the more I felt the need to punish myself for being such a worthless entity. I scratched at my wrists with plastic pink razors, too scared to really go deep. I was jealous of Nina, who could make such deep beautiful gashes with real knives in her arms. Blood made me squeamish; I didn't have what it took to be a cutter.

One day after walking home from the city bus following a particularly lonely day at school, I slammed the front door shut, ran into the kitchen, and flung open the freezer. I pulled out the half-gallon carton of cookie dough ice cream and set it on the counter. Then I opened the refrigerator and grabbed the tray of chocolate frosted brownies. Found a spoon. Inhaled, exhaled, inhaled, exhaled, then tore everything open, a panting animal, ready to attack.

Spoon into ice cream carton, glob of ice cream on spoon, spoon into brownie tray, glob of brownie onto ice cream on spoon. Spoon dripping brownie and ice cream all over the counter, my shirt, and the floor on its way into my mouth. Creamy brown goo oozed out the corners of my mouth, all over my hands. But I kept going, hovering hypnotized over the counter. Bite. Taste. Chew. Swallow. Bite. Taste. Chew. Swallow. Painful pressure on my belly. Empty head. Quiet house.

This became my ritual. Nearly every day I came home, shaking with anticipation, then devoured cookies, ice cream, brownies, cereal, peanut butter, donuts, whatever I could find in the kitchen. Afterwards, I was always disgusted. I ran to the mirror immediately to cringe at my reflection. I wanted to scrape off my face, take a hacksaw to my stomach. My bones felt like jail cell bars. I dug my nails into my forearms, bit down hard into the skin above my bicep, slammed my arms and legs into walls.

When the school year finally ended, camp was a welcome reprieve, but in the fall I started high school, and all the bad feelings rushed back in, sharper than before. Walking across the quad at lunch, watching the various group interactions with a sinking feeling in my stomach, I craved a way to stand out, excel, to prove I was talented, prove I was lovable.

I soon discovered what would bring the attention.

"Oh, my God, you're like, so skinny. Do you, like, eat or whatever?" girls in the locker room started saying, staring at me while we suited up for Phys Ed.

"Yes," I said self-consciously. And I *was* eating. I had always been thin, inhabiting a particularly skinny pair of legs. My thighs never touched, and my lower legs and ankles were especially bony. At five feet, four inches I weighed ninety-five pounds. But until high school, when weight became every girl's obsession, no one had commented on my physique. Suddenly hearing "you're so skinny," over and over began to have a strangely intoxicating effect: It was tinged with praise and jealousy. Desperate for friends, I thought, *I know, I'll get even skinnier. Then I'll get more praise, more jealousy, and maybe then people will love me.* I stopped eating to see if anyone would notice, to give myself a purpose, to punish myself for feeling and wanting so much. I told myself I was worthless and didn't deserve food until someone told me otherwise.

To motivate myself, I spent my nights compulsively making collages of emaciated women in magazines, primarily from *Vogue*. Sometimes I cut out the whole woman in whatever skimpy outfit she was wearing, her collarbones like handlebars. Other times, I just cut out a part of the woman, say, the lips, coated in vamp red lipstick. Or the eye: blue or green or brown with heavy strokes of color above and below, like circus face paint. Sometimes the whole head: powder-white skin and frizzy teased hair, hair like my mother's. She brushed out her Jewish red hair until it was huge. My father always told her to straighten it, thin it. But *Vogue's* women made hair like that sexy. They could wear a giant trash bag over their fleshless rib cages, flared-out hips, knobby knees, slap on some stilettos, and people would muse over this provocative image of high fashion. Of all the magazines, I was most intrigued by *Vogue*, where the models were most skeletal, the fashion strangest, the pictures promoting a depressed heroin-chic woman. I cut out legs, torsos, feet, arms, hands, noses, eyes, heads, lips, whole bodies, layering them on top of each other until I'd plastered a Picasso-like arrangement across my entire ceiling. Staring at it from my bed as I wriggled my way into sleep night after night, I vowed to follow these women's lead.

I ate nothing for breakfast and two small apples for lunch. Two small ones were more psychologically soothing than one big one because I could drag the experience out longer. I would think about these apples all through my first four periods. At lunch, I took tiny bites, savoring each one, eating every bit of the apple until it was just core and two thin strings from top to bottom. I would suck on the core until I was sure I'd extracted every last bit of flavor. Then off to fifth period, where it was time to daydream about the next thing: one nonfat Yoplait yogurt when I got home from school. This was my only chance for flavor variety, as I had strawberry, apricot, mango, banana. *What will it be today?* I'd salivate thinking about it, body whining. I told my body to shut up; it was weak, I was stronger. I would win. When I finally got home to the yogurt, first I licked the lid. I collected small dabs at the edge of my spoon, which I sucked hard, savoring for as long as possible, one teensy bite after another until I reached the bottom of the plastic container. I scraped the bottom with the spoon and licked it long after all had been consumed, spooning empty air, sucking with all my might. Then I weighed myself. I congratulated myself as the pounds fell off: ninety, eighty-five, eighty. I beamed with pride at my discipline. I'd step off the scale and head to my room to do homework and wait for dinner. When I wasn't eating, I was chewing Extra peppermint gum, usually a new piece every hour. My jaw always ached.

At that time, my father was serving himself small portions of whatever my mom prepared for dinner and then piling a mountain of salad on top of it. My mom, brother, and sister lapped up all food voraciously without reserve. But my dinner was always the same: a small baked potato, broccoli, salad with nonfat dressing, and a Diet Coke. Occasionally, I added a few spoonfuls of dry tuna.

Like my father, I let myself have as much salad as possible because it had practically no calories. My mom dismissed my eating habits as a phase, some teenage diet that she believed would pass. But my father was visibly uncomfortable every time we ate together, aware that my eating habits had become similar to his. He wouldn't speak to me, but stared at my plate across the table while we both chomped our lettuce like zombies. I pretended not to notice.

As my body changed, I felt more powerful. At night, I closed my eyes in bed and ran my hands along my bony protuberances. I placed my fingers on the jutting base of my sternum, then slowly dragged my hands outward, tracing each nearly unearthed rib. Hands roamed downward, resting on hipbones like coat hooks. My fingers glided across the outside of my bony, fleshless thighs up the insides until they met in the crevice between, resting. No response. Hands back down to the knees, two giant knobs. Back up the sides and underneath to the top of my pelvis: knobs there, too. A place that got sore if I ever lay on a hardwood floor. Likewise, sitting on a hard surface was often painful, grinding into the bones at my seat. I touched those as well as I lay in bed, eyes closed. My hands swirled up and down my body. Soon I grew irritated. My body was hungry. I told it to shut up. *Hungry. Shut up. Hungry. I'm sorry, did you not hear me? I said, shut up! Shut up! Shut up!* I punched my stomach for being such a baby. It no longer had any say. I was in charge. I always looked forward to the moment just before sleep, when I'd become too tired to care anymore. Likewise, waking was the lowest point of the day; I'd grown resentful of consciousness.

I couldn't see that I was largely responsible for my isolation. I alienated myself from my peers and my family, living a self-fulfilling prophecy. Since I hid at lunch, participated in no extracurricular activities, ran to my room, and shut the door after school, no one had a chance to talk to me. What I wanted more than anything was for someone to reach out, but no one did. Because my parents never said anything, I assumed they didn't care. After six months, I was cold all the time, and my hair was falling out. While all the girls around me were developing breasts and getting their periods, my chest was still completely flat, and I'd never had a period. My skin took on a translucent purple glow. I drowned myself in baggy sweatshirts to hide my bony frame, becoming nearly invisible. I was caving in, days bleeding one into the next, floating through half-conscious, hardly speaking, hardly moving, sitting in one place and staring for long periods of time. The more weight I lost, the heavier I actually felt.

One day in Phys Ed, I participated in a physical evaluation. The teachers recorded how many pull-ups, push-ups, sit-ups we could do, timed our miles, measured our body fat, and weighed us. I was seventy-five pounds.

"Wow, that's really light," the teacher noted, "Are you eating?"

I paused a moment, then said, "Yes," hoping she would be concerned and challenge me, force me to eat something, then hug me and let me cry on her shoulder for the rest of the morning. I was so hungry, dizzy, and cold. Barely able to stand, I thought I might break.

"Okay...next!" she called out, and I stepped off the scale, heading back to the locker room to slip my gnarled limbs back inside my baggy uniform and wade ghostlike through the rest of the day. It seemed like no one would ever notice.

About a month later, I got a pass to go to the counselor's office. I didn't know what I was in trouble for. When I entered, she had her hands clasped on her desk. The room didn't have any windows. It smelled like musty old books. The woman wore glasses. Her hair was short, frizzy, and brown.

"Have a seat," she said.

I sat down, my mouth zipped shut.

"How are you?" she asked.

"I'm okay."

She frowned and took a deep breath. "A concerned friend came in here yesterday and said she doesn't think you are eating. Is this true?"

A frog turned a somersault in my throat. My cheeks got hot, my eyes watered. "Yes." Someone had noticed. I felt so grateful.

"Are you going to tell your parents?"

I couldn't imagine just flat out telling my parents. I wanted them to figure it out on their own.

"Do you want me to call and have a conversation with them first?" she asked.

I really did want them to know. And once they found out, I wanted them to take turns hugging me and holding me like they did when I was a small child, to tell me they were so sorry they hadn't been there, that they loved me more than anything. I had cut myself off emotionally from them for so long; I missed them so much. I shut my eyes and pictured the two of them sitting at the table across from me, talking about all this later that evening. *I'm so sorry; I love you so much. Please love me back. Please don't make me grow up; please protect me forever.*

I opened my eyes. "Okay."

She sent me back to class. First, I went to the bathroom and looked in the mirror. I was trying to look into myself, to really see myself from the outside. I wasn't sure who that was. My dyed black hair was frayed and frizzy, looked almost gray under the light in a messy ball on the top of my head. Face pale and sunken in. Bulging gray-blue eyes. I dug my nails into my arms. Then I chucked one of my lunch apples onto the bathroom floor. Mushy bits flew. I wasn't sure what was about to happen, but I was ready for a change.

My mom, who always did everything in her power to solve problems through practical measures, steered me to a nutritionist and an adolescent physician specializing in eating disorders. I knew I should eat, thought about food constantly, and understood intellectually that gaining weight was necessary. But I couldn't eat; the force denying me food felt like demonic possession. Whereas before I thought I had been the one in control, I began to see that anorexia had always been this parasite. It wouldn't let me follow the meal plan my nutritionist and I had worked out.

At family dinner, my parents begged me to eat, and I threw a fit. Crying and screaming like a three-year-old, I wailed in protest, "I don't want to! I can't! Leave me alone!" I ran to my room and locked the door. My parents knocked and yelled, "Get out here right now!" "No!" I yelled back, hysterical. After ten or fifteen minutes of this back and forth, tears dried, force slightly drained, when my parents were no longer yelling but begging, I crawled to the door, marched back to the table, and ate a full plate of dinner, bite after bite, parents watching, whole family silent. My twelve-year-old sister and eight-year-old brother sat, dumbfounded, not quite sure how to react or what to do. I always assumed they resented me; I was ashamed of being such a bad example. At the same time, I resented them for being able to eat without a problem. They seemed so well-adjusted. Why did I have to be the freakish, flailing older sister?

One night, long after Tiffany and Austin had finished their dinner and retreated to their rooms to do homework, my parents continued to sit with me while I struggled to finish my chicken and potatoes. My mom was patient, encouraging me sweetly to please eat, determined to sit beside me as long as it took to finish. My father, however, sat across from me, staring at me in disgust, silently fuming. Finally, he broke. "You are so selfish," he snapped, "Ruining the family by draining so much energy from us over this crap!" A rage bomb detonated in the center of my chest. The blood rushed to my face, creating such intense pressure that my head felt like it might actually blow off my neck. I dropped my fork, stood up, and flung my chair into the side of the table.

"*I'm* ruining the family? Are you fucking kidding me?" I ran to my room, slammed the door, threw myself on the bed, and cried violently into my pillow, banging the wall with my fists. Then I heard a quiet knock on my door.

"What?" I screamed.

The door creaked open slowly as I wiped my wet cheeks and tried to catch my breath. There was my dad, leaning against the doorframe, looking at me with soft eyes. He had completely transformed.

"Do you want to go for a walk?" he asked. Then, a few moments later, "I'm really sorry for what I said."

I stared back at him for a long time. "Okay," I said finally, exhaling a long sigh and dragging myself up to stand. My throat hurt from screaming.

"Okay," he said and turned. I followed him down the hall and through the kitchen, where my mom was washing the dinner dishes. He held the front door open for me, and I stepped under his arm into the early evening twilight, planted my feet, and turned back to watch the door swing shut behind him. We began walking side by side in stiff silence, moving slowly due to the poor circulation in his leg. Neither of us looked at the other. Instead, I tried to see inside the windows of the houses we passed. I wondered what other families were like, what other fathers were like, what kinds of relationships they had with their daughters. I listened to my father's heavy breathing until it became the only sound in the world. I imagined the inside of his lungs; they probably looked like the smokers' lungs I saw in my health book at school, part inflamed, part black and shriveled. As he dragged his leg along, I thought about his heart working so hard to pump fresh blood into his clogged arteries. I thought about his body straining to perform its basic functions. I considered what I'd done to my body and realized I was partially attempting to emulate him.

"You know, it's too bad you never got to meet Grandpa Irving." His voice startled me out of my trance. "You really would have liked each other."

Irving had been a well-respected rabbi in Woodmere, Long Island, where my father grew up. Irving was a powerful orator and highly intelligent man; my father admired him but had always felt small in his shadow.

"Oh, why?"

"He was intelligent and complex, and a strong personality like you. I think you would have had a lot to talk about."

As he spoke, I felt my breathing slow and the muscles in my face soften. I drew closer to him and gently bumped his shoulder. I looked up at the sky, clouds thinning out inside a deepening blue. The air was getting cooler. I pulled my sweatshirt sleeves over my hands and shivered lightly.

"You know who else you're like?" he asked.

"Who?"

"Me," he said, looking away.

"I know."

We understood each other deeply, on a level that transcended words. Each successive footstep dissolved a little more of the barrier between us. We walked under a dome of oceanic blue sky right before nightfall. A sliver of moon. His labored breathing. When we returned to the house, he gave me a giant generous hug. I melted into his chest and stomach and loved him.

I continued wrestling with myself, but ultimately made little progress in the months that followed. I'd gain two pounds, then lose three. So addicted to not eating and so uncomfortable with the sensation of being full, I could barely eat at meals. My nutritionist prescribed Ensure Plus, an eight-ounce liquid dietary supplement with three hundred and sixty calories. It comes in vanilla, strawberry, and chocolate, but mostly tastes like flavored Milk of Magnesia. I was supposed to drink one, then two, then three a day, in addition to eating three meals, but I would open the can, take a sip, and pour the rest out. At night, I cried in bed and filled pages of journals, promising myself the next day was a fresh start. Then the next day arrived and ended up just like the last.

In the meantime, summer was approaching. Camp loomed on the visible horizon. I really wanted to go, believing that if I could just get to camp, everything would be okay. It was the most healing place I could imagine. I was going to be in the oldest age group and had been looking forward to this summer since my first, as the oldest kids were by far the coolest. My parents had worked out a scholarship big enough for me to spend two sessions, eight weeks. But my doctor told me that I would have to show serious signs of weight gain, or I wouldn't be able to go. This was the motivation I needed. The weekend before the first session, with my mom as my devout partner and cheerleader, I turned into a vacuum, sucking up everything in sight. I gained five pounds in three days and, at eighty pounds, was allowed to go. My doctor made a deal with the camp nurse: I had to be weighed every morning and drink a nutritional supplement under her supervision.

Sitting beside my sister as the bus turned off the main street in Ojai and rolled slowly down the narrow road next to avocado and orange groves, I saw the sign that said, "Camp Ramah," and my eyes welled up with tears. Tiffany saw me tearing up and didn't say anything. She and I hadn't spoken much in a long time. She leaned over and kissed my cheek, the world's softest kiss. Without speaking, I hugged her. She hugged me back. I felt like I had been saved.

I got off the bus and fell into the arms of all my best friends: Celia, Jessica, Nicole, Sarah. They each squeezed me tightly. As they stepped back from our embrace and actually took me in, I could see they were a bit startled by my appearance, but trying not to make it obvious.

"Let's go!" said Nicole. "We're all in Tent Fourteen!" We lugged our bags up the hill, found our tent, claimed our beds, and began to unpack. It was sweltering, and I was feeling dizzy but tried to ignore it.

"Oh, my God, did you guys see Aaron?" Celia said, tucking her short hair behind her ear. "He got so cute this year, I am totally going to try to hook up with him."

We all laughed as we pulled T-shirts from our duffle bags, folded them, and stacked them on the wooden shelves.

Then Jessica pulled out a giant plastic Ziploc bag full of mini chocolate chip cookies, Hershey bars, and red vines. She dangled it in the air.

"Anyone?" she called out.

"Oh, hell yeah!" shouted Sarah, pulling her long red hair up into a ponytail. Everyone stopped unpacking and congregated on

Jessica's bed. I followed and sat down last, eyeing the treats nervously. Jessica busted open the bag and everyone partook greedily, continuing to talk about boys they hoped to hook up with, how unbelievable it was that we were finally in the oldest age group, how awesome this summer was going to be. But after a while, I faded everything out, unable to concentrate on anything but the food they were so carefree about sharing. Jessica held the bag out to me, offering. I plucked a single mini cookie and brought it to my lips, then opened my mouth and took the smallest possible bite. I could barely even taste it, the bite was so small. I knew I would have to finish that cookie. What I really wanted to do was hold onto it until we all got up and then throw it away. But this would definitely seem weird. So I ate the whole thing as fast as I could to get it over with. Then I felt guilty. I imagined spontaneously sprouting a belt of flab around my middle. I sized up my friends' bodies. They were eating this junk without a second thought, and they all looked great. I berated myself for thinking the way I did and for being distracted from the conversation by this bullshit.

Finally Jessica sealed the bag, got up, and hid it behind her stack of shirts, and I relaxed. I was able to pay attention to what they were saying just fine after that, chimed in and laughed along. I was so happy to be in their company. This *was* going to be an awesome summer.

That afternoon, we gathered under a tree on the hill to learn our group song. The oldest age group had the longest, most fun song, and was the only group that got to run into the center of the main hall to sing it, and people got super into it. We sang it that night after dinner and I felt euphoric.

For the first few days, everything felt great, as long as there was no food around. Meals were hell; I continued to freeze up and socially disengage until the food was gone. I was really having a hard time making myself eat; the force that possessed me was powerful. I would peel the cheese off my pizza, scoop tomato sauce on my finger, and suck it while the rest of my tent mates devoured their third or fourth slices. I imagined an invisible wall erecting itself between them and myself during meals, not considering that they actually noticed my behavior the whole time. Also, I somehow convinced the nurse that I didn't need to be watched while drinking my morning supplement because she made me nervous. I don't know why she let me off the hook; I threw that crap out every single morning.

By the middle of the week, meals aside, everything didn't feel so great anymore. I never had any energy. The average temperature at camp is near one hundred degrees and the campgrounds require a decent amount of walking. These two factors made it almost impossible for me to participate in most outdoor activities without feeling like I was going to keel over. By the end of the first week, I weighed seventy-seven pounds.

One of the privileges of being in the oldest age group was going on a weeklong camping trip with hiking and sleeping in nature. I would never be able to make it through the trip, being far too weak and having lost too much weight as it was, never mind what I would lose by hiking. My counselors called an emergency meeting into order with the camp doctor, themselves, and me.

We sat in an office in the infirmary around a table. The room had one small window at the top of one wall. The doctor had gray hair, glasses, and kind eyes. I had a lump in my throat the size of the table; I could barely swallow. We all sat for nearly a minute of thick silence until the doctor finally leaned toward me and broke it.

"So, Amanda, how are you enjoying your summer so far?"

I looked past him. "Um, it's okay."

He shifted his weight in his seat and leaned back. I hugged my knees to my chest and dug my top teeth into my bottom lip.

"You've been losing weight."

"Yeah…" I said, lobbing my gaze up to the window.

"Well…what do you want to do? Do you want to stay at camp?"

I was shocked that this was being posed as a question. I'd assumed he was going to scold me, ask me what the hell was wrong with me, why couldn't I just eat? It wasn't that hard. People had to eat to live. And if I was so weak that I couldn't snap out of it, then I deserved to be kicked out of camp. But these were actually my own cruel thoughts. His tone was kind, like his eyes.

I knew I was in need of serious therapy, and that camp was not solving my problems the way I had hoped. My heart sank. My fingers and toes tingled. Pressure mounted in my chest and throat. Tears pooled in the corners of my eyes. I blinked them down my cheeks and erupted, "I want to go home and get this thing out of me." I folded my arms on the table, dropped my head down, and had the hardest cry of my life. My counselor, Rena, pulled her chair closer to mine and rubbed my bony back in soothing gentle circles. It felt so relieving to be touched, and it made me cry harder.

The camp doctor called my doctor in San Diego to get his opinion. Without a moment's hesitation, he insisted that I leave. Then my parents were called. They would be picking me up the next morning. So it was settled. I continued to stare at the window as I listened to the camp doctor's side of these conversations, but because it was so high, all I could see was a small square of blue sky.

"Do you want to tell the rest of the girls in the tent yourself?" Rena asked me. "Or do you want me to tell them?"

"I'll tell them," I said, sitting up, wiping my wet splotchy face. "I'll tell them I have to leave for family reasons." As if they didn't know the truth. I was so embarrassed and ashamed; I felt like a disgusting diseased creature.

After the night activity, Rena brought all the girls from our tent into one of the multi-purpose rooms. We sat down in a circle and I looked at each of those thirteen faces, many of them my closest friends in the world. Inhaling as deeply as my fleshless ribs would allow, I said, "I have to leave tomorrow. I am going home... for family reasons. I have to go home." Silence. Everyone looked stunned. Nobody spoke. Soon, everyone began to cry. It was shocking; I was so moved that people cared this much about me.

"Girls, let's go back to the tent and help Amanda pack," said Rena. We left the room together and proceeded to walk up the hill to our tent. "The hill" is considered a sacred place, the center of camp. We all stopped in the middle of the hill, and suddenly everyone was hugging me. Thirteen bodies huddled around my paper-thin figure. Hands reaching for me, squeezing my arms, shoulders, legs. Hands rubbing my back. Hands on my head. Sounds of crying. Sounds of breath catching. Chests heaving. Bodies shaking, pressed together. We stood there in the moonlight, a twenty-eight-legged and -armed sniffling creature. The grass was wet. It smelled like trees.

We stayed up all night, crying, laughing, taking pictures, playing music, and packing my things. My friend decided to make a tape for me to listen to once I had left camp. Everyone took turns going outside to record a special message, sing songs, recall inside jokes, whatever they felt inclined to do. I was incredibly grateful for this, as it would keep me company through whatever lay ahead.

After we had been packing and hanging out for a while, everyone started munching on their secret candy stashes and offering me some. I declined as usual, but then a force within me rose up and, for a brief moment, squashed the repressive demon. Damn it, some of my best camp memories were of conversations shared over candy on friends' beds after lights out. This was my last night with them ever, my summer was ruined, I had no idea what the next day was going to bring, and I wanted some fucking candy. I turned back to Celia. "I changed my mind. Can I have some?" She flashed a huge bittersweet smile and said, "Of course." I coated my tongue with milk chocolate, strawberry sour belts, and red licorice, and it actually brought tears to my eyes; it was like a revelation, it all tasted so good, so sweet. I knew this was a fleeting moment of indulgence. I would wake up in the morning and be racked with guilt. I shoved these thoughts aside. *Please let me have this one night.* I fell asleep in my clothes and dreamt about floating on a boat down a chocolate river, my friends all around me kissing my cheeks, holding my hands.

In the morning, I went into my sister's tent and woke her up to say goodbye. Then at around 8:30 a.m., my parents' car pulled up next to the patch of grass where I was sitting with friends. My father got out and loaded the car with my bags, then returned to the driver's seat next to my brother. No one looked at me or said anything as I climbed into the back seat next to my mom. I folded up inside the weighted silence as my father drove.

"We're taking you to the hospital," my father informed me.

"Why?"

"Because that's what we have to do," he said, eyes fixed on the road in front of him.

I began to cry softly as I sat there for a second, staring at my hands, then unzipped my backpack and pulled out the tape my friends had made me. I stood up and extended my arm through the front seats, slipping the tape into the tape deck.

"I love you, Amanda. Thank you for always being there for me. I would like to think I've always been there for you. I'm sorry if I haven't."

"Amanda, be strong. Know that you're beautiful. Try not to get too sad. I love you."

Once we were on the freeway and had listened to several depressing messages and songs from friends, a knotted ball of rage began to fester beneath my sternum. I was infuriated with myself, and this internal monster that I allowed to control me. The ball was getting bigger and bigger, expanding down to my stomach, up my back. How could this be happening? What was this demonic creature inside of me? Once we were on the freeway, I lost it. Sobbing in the back seat next to my mother, at eighty miles per hour, I flung open the car door and screamed, "I hate myself! I want to kill myself!"

"Stop it!" my mom shrieked at me, her fingers wrapping tightly around my arm. I wriggled out of her grasp violently to free myself. She grabbed me again with her left hand, saving me from flying out in front of a bus zooming by, and slammed the door with her right.

My father turned around in the driver's seat and screamed, "Don't you think it breaks our hearts to have to do this?" I was shocked to witness his steadily streaming tears. It was the first time I had ever seen my father cry.

Austin sat unresponsive in the front seat.

I slumped down, closed my eyes, and tried to breathe.

When we got to the hospital, replete with white walls and pale people in hospital gowns pushing I.V. poles, I started to feel sick to my stomach. I peaked into the open rooms as my parents and brother walked me down the hall to the nurse's station. I didn't see anyone else my age, mostly older people who really looked sick. I shuddered and ground my teeth hard. A nurse checked me in at the desk and guided me to my room. She showed me where my hospital gown was and told me to put it on. It suddenly occurred to me that I was a real hospital patient, and I was terrified. My family sat down on the visitor chairs while I went into the bathroom to change. I noted the electric scale by the toilet. When I opened the door, the nurse came toward me, holding a clipboard. "Please step on the scale," she said. I stepped on and looked down as the number appeared: 77.3. The nurse noted this on her clipboard. She extended the clipboard toward me as I stepped off. "Please sign this," she said, tightening her brown ponytail.

I sat down on the bed and read the words at the top of the page: **Treatment Plan For:** *Amanda Miller.* **Diagnosis**: *Anorexia Nervosa.* **Current weight**: *77 pounds.* **Goal weight**: *90–95 pounds.* My temples were pounding as my eyes darted across the page word to word until the letters began spiraling together. 1. *Patient will be weighed once daily, in a hospital gown, before breakfast and after voiding.* 2. *Nutritional supplements will be used to provide patient with the necessary caloric intake to allow for weight gain of 1.0 pound over three days.* 3. **Activity Level:** *Bed rest with bathroom privileges. Bathroom unlocked.* 4. **Goals for this admission:** *Weight gain of 1–2 pounds, normal blood pressure and temperature, understanding of severity of illness.*

I scrawled my name at the bottom of the page, handed the clipboard back to the nurse, and stared at her for a second. She had a sweet, tired face.

"We'll need to draw blood to check your electrolyte levels."

I scanned my parents' faces. They both made feeble attempts at smiling. My brother was looking at the ceiling, bored. I looked back at the nurse, mumbled a quiet "okay," and held out my arm. She had to try several times before she found a vein that worked. With every prick, my stomach flipped. When she finally hit the good vein, it took forever to get the blood out. I cried silently while my family stared. I felt like such a freak. Shortly after the blood was taken, I had an I.V. site inserted into a vein on the top of my hand that could be hooked up to an I.V. if necessary. It would remain in my vein until I left the hospital because, at any moment, a doctor could find it necessary to feed me intravenously if I refused to eat or was throwing up my food. The I.V. site insertion was far worse than having blood drawn. The nurse had to tunnel the needle really deep into a vein before she realized that it wasn't going to work. She did that with three or four veins before she found that the one on the top of my left hand was responding.

I felt queasy and lightheaded, tears soaking my cheeks as I squeezed my father's hand. He was more patient and supportive of me than he had been in my entire life. My mother was her usual warm presence. As for my brother, his boredom dissipated during the needle insertions as he realized something was wrong, though he couldn't process it fully. The nurse left and returned with a chocolate Ensure, which I sipped while they sat with me. No one had anything to say and I was really tired, so I asked them to go. They each kissed me goodbye and got up to leave. My father lingered a moment after the other two stepped out, looked at me for a long a time, and finally said, "Please call if you need anything."

I shot an exhausted half smile his way. "I will."

Then he slipped out, and I fell hard into a long, deep sleep. When I woke, there was a letter from Tiffany on my nightstand on bright yellow stationery: "I hope you're eating lots of pancakes and stuff so you can come back to camp. I love you."

The nights at the hospital were the loneliest. I would lie awake, listening to the tape my friends had made me on "Repeat." After a while, their words and voices started to blend together. *"Amanda, I love you... Try not to get too sad... Amanda, I... You're beautiful... Amanda, remember when... I, Amanda... Thank you for... I'm sorry... strength... Amanda."* Listening to my name over and over in other people's mouths began to reaffirm my identity. I was a whole person, with people who cared about me; I was worthy of life. "I love you, I love you," the messages kept saying. I cried thick hot tears, flooded with gratitude; I was loved after all. As I soaked up this reality, I was determined to obliterate the snarling beast inside me.

I was discharged from the hospital after five days and began a rigorous outpatient regime: group and individual therapy and nutritional counseling. In group therapy, I was hesitant to share at first, but the openness and willingness of those around me was empowering. "The sensation of being full after meals makes me shake," I remember one of the girls saying. "If I eat what I think is too much one day, I'll make up for it by hardly eating at all the next." Another shared, in tears, "I just feel so ugly all the time." I could relate to everything. This echo became a cushion of support, relief. Before long, everything that I'd felt and experienced was flooding out of me, draining the oppressive force by which I'd been possessed for so long. Now that I felt understood and validated, my confidence was returning.

I was motivated to actually follow the meal plan my nutritionist and I worked out. We gradually increased my caloric intake; it was a slow but steady process. There were whole days when I didn't feel possessed at all and wasn't worrying about fat content or weighing myself every day. Then there were days when I struggled and relapsed. But group therapy was helping me to learn patience, and teaching me that this was something to work at every day. The support I'd been lacking and craving for so long was propelling me forward.

My individual therapist suggested we try some family therapy sessions. However, these sessions were largely unproductive. My siblings were unreceptive. My sister never spoke. At one point, the therapist asked my brother, "Have you noticed any changes at family meals?"

"Well, my sister Tiffany and I just got braces, and they make our teeth sore, so we have to eat softer foods and stuff. Also, food gets stuck in the braces a lot."

My mother was open to family therapy, wanted to do whatever possible to see me through recovery. But my father was resistant. He never said anything during sessions. If the therapist asked him a question, he would give a one-word response. He looked at the floor, exhaling tension into the room. It made me angry; wasn't he supposed to be the mature adult? We stopped going to family therapy after just a few sessions.

As I got stronger, my father's health deteriorated. I gained weight. He ate more lettuce, smoked more cigarettes. The more he withdrew, the more I resented his behavior, the exact behavior I was struggling to destroy in myself. His temper aroused my temper, and we'd find ourselves in yelling matches over trivial things like my not saying "good morning" after he'd muttered it too low for me to hear. He came to embody everything I did not want to be: a gloomy hermit in a hole.

To force myself out of my shell, in the second semester of tenth grade, I decided to take drama at school. In class, I immediately befriended people who shared my intensity. Surprisingly quickly, performing became the ideal venue for me to channel all my emotional energy. Standing on a stage ignited my adrenaline, the character's emotion pulsing through me, my voice powerful and resonant.

In the beginning of eleventh grade, I performed in my first play, double cast as the Music Master in Moliere's *The Would-Be*

Gentleman. I loved how the cast bonded as we rehearsed every day, spending long hours together, becoming our own little family. I loved the excitement of opening night, putting on our costumes and makeup in our dressing rooms, standing in a circle before curtain, passing a pulse from hand to hand to prove our support for one another.

On opening night, the other girl played the Music Master while I played her student composer, a comedic character who never spoke and got distracted by her own fantastical world while the Music Master was trying to teach her. One of my gags was experimenting with all the things the conductor's baton could be used for besides conducting. I used it as a walking stick, a back scratcher, and finally a sword, which engrossed me the most. Then when the Music Master turned around to ensure I was listening and following along, I promptly quit whatever I was doing and pretended to be paying attention. She scolded me for my tomfoolery and returned to the lesson, and I again got distracted. I was completely engrossed in the imagined reality. My adrenaline was pumping, the lights were hot on my face, and the audience was clapping and laughing wildly at my ridiculous antics. I had never felt so high in my life.

After the show, my cast mates all hugged me and told me how funny I was. Then, once I had changed and come outside, audience members stopped to shake my hand and told me I was their favorite actor in the whole show. I had no lines and had only been on stage for one tiny scene at the very beginning. I was elated. I passed through the crowd of strangers and found my family, my mother holding a big bouquet of flowers. They all hugged and kissed me.

We went to dinner at *TGI Friday's* to celebrate. I ordered a turkey sandwich, French fries and a Coke, eating everything without even an ounce of guilt. My dad picked at a salad, but I pretended not to notice. This was *my* big night. As I ate, I talked a mile a minute about how excited I was for the next show, even though I didn't yet know what it would be. I was completely smitten with theater. My future was bright, and the food was delicious.

Your Particular Smile

My father's head bobbed up and down as he nearly collapsed face first into his untouched spaghetti. He jerked up with a start. "Oh, God, oh, God," he muttered, and dropped his head into his hands. My brother, sister, mother, and I continued to eat, vacantly reporting the events of our days, unable to deny the thickness in the air, the anxiety we all felt about the sick man at our table. The radiation therapy to his lungs and brain earlier in the day had made him fatigued and dizzy. At the same time, his body was straining to metabolize a smorgasbord of medications. Steroids to open the radiated air passageways in his lungs, making him woozy and puffy. An appetite stimulant. Anti-nausea pills. Vicodin for pain. Coumadin: a blood thinner. He had to inject himself with shots twice a day to loosen the blood clots in his legs; his feet were usually blue and swollen and needed to be iced.

"Could you please pass the sauce?" my mom asked me.

"Sauce, sauce. I want salami," my father said to no one in particular, eyes vacant, face drained.

Austin stabbed at his tomato chunks. "I caught a fly ball at baseball today."

My father leaned his head back in his chair and stared at the ceiling, breathing audibly. His effortful breathing transitioned into forceful coughing, as if his lungs were straining to eject themselves from his body.

"I got an A on my history test," Tiffany said, staring deep into her plate.

"That's great," my mother said, "And how was your day?" she asked me, glancing vaguely in my direction.

"It was okay." Realizing I had twirled way too much spaghetti around my fork to fit in my mouth, I dropped the fork and sighed. I really didn't feel like talking; I was too uncomfortable with the drugged-out patient to my left, masquerading as my father. He had fallen asleep in his chair.

He was fifty-three and had just been diagnosed with lung cancer. The cancer was identified at Stage Four, meaning it had metastasized to other parts of the body, in his case, the brain. Stage Four is the most difficult to treat, and a patient's survival prognosis is typically eight months to a year. My father's doctor predicted he had six months.

Cancer was the death ticket he'd been waiting for. Maybe it was his chemical constitution. Maybe he never got over being adopted. Maybe he never found his niche in life. So heavy he could never quite lift himself up, couldn't release the tension in his jaw, his shoulders, sit outside and enjoy the sun, couldn't relax. Life seemed to fit him like a straitjacket. He wanted out.

There was no fight, no "I shall overcome," no "this will make me stronger." Just "goodbye, everyone; Death, I'm waiting," and "if it wouldn't be too much trouble, could you please come in my sleep." Upon diagnosis, he transitioned quickly into a dying man. Within weeks, he had aged decades, taken to his bed, hooked himself up to a do-it-yourself-at-home oxygen tank, which took on the specter of a severed appendage. I was seventeen and beginning my senior year of high school. As I watched my father dissolve inside his sheets, I began applying to colleges for acting.

At the end of September, two weeks after his diagnosis, we attended Rosh Hashanah services. Rosh Hashanah, the Jewish New Year, kicks off the high holidays, the holiest days in the Jewish calendar. Supposedly, God opens up His giant book of life and starts inscribing everyone's fate in it, based on their actions of the previous year. During the ten days between Rosh Hashanah and Yom Kippur, the day of repentance, God is watching to see how many Jews are repenting hard enough to warrant reversal of his severe decrees. My father and I were the only members of my family in synagogue that day. My siblings were outside with their friends, while my mother was leading the children's service.

On Rosh Hashanah it is inscribed,
And on Yom Kippur it is sealed.
How many shall pass away and how many shall be born,
Who shall live and who shall die…

I stood with my father as these words were read aloud. Both of us kept silent. Somewhere mid-reading, I saw tears falling from his eyes. At first, they trickled lightly, and then streamed steadily down his sunken cheeks. This was the second time in my life I had seen him cry. I instinctively put my arm around him and quickly turned my head away, not wanting to witness his breakdown. Abruptly, my cheeks were wet with tears of my own.

Who shall reach the end of his days and who shall not,
Who shall perish by water and who by fire…

"I wish my father were here," he said, "I really miss him." But his father had been dead for eighteen years. Reflexively, I began rubbing his back, something I had never done before. It felt forced and foreign for me to be comforting him in this way. For the rest of the recitation, we stood together in silence. Then it ended and we sat down.

Once, in the middle of the night, I woke up to go to the bathroom and heard him crying softly in the dark living room. He had taken to sleeping in a chair because lying down restricted his breathing and was bad for his circulation. I went in and sat on the couch across from him, studying his silhouette. I thought about hugging him, but my arms felt paralyzed, like steel weights. Shivering in the midnight draft, I held my breath, nausea and anxiety swirling beneath my sternum.

"I want to see you graduate," he said, still crying.

He was unraveling. As death grew more plausible, he was becoming afraid. Still, my conscious mind couldn't process what he was saying. I was supposed to graduate that year. Wouldn't he make it until then? How much time did he have left? I wanted him to see me have a career, marry, have children. He was going to miss all of it. There was still so much we hadn't talked about, conversations I had not been mature enough to have about philosophy, politics, literature, history, things I knew he cared deeply about. I just assumed he would always be there, that once I was an adult, we would be closer. I hugged him, burying my face in his chest for several breaths, then, still unsure as to what to say, tiptoed back to my room and cried quietly in my bed, unable to sleep much the rest of the night.

Early in November, I performed my first leading role in my high school's production of Jean Anouilh's French farce, *Ring Round the Moon*. In the program, I dedicated my performance to my father. When I came backstage, I thanked the various audience members I passed for their compliments and looked around to find my family. Finally, I spotted them and gazed at my father, his hair thinned and gray, face exhausted from radiation, eyes beaming. I ran to him and threw my arms around his waist.

"You've really come so far, I'm so proud of you," he said, hugging me tightly. It was the first time he'd ever spoken those words. As the fluorescent overhead lights beat down on us, people and their voices swarming through the space, I closed my eyes, blocking out the light, letting the background noise congeal into a steady hum. His words pulsed through my body: ears to chest to fingertips.

"I love you, Dad."

"I love you, too," he said.

On the night of Thanksgiving, he got out of bed, showered, and ate a full meal after weeks of hardly eating or moving. Maybe something had shifted within him; maybe he would surprise everyone with his newfound desire to live.

Upon waking the next morning, I headed straight for the kitchen and nervously stuffed myself with Entenmann's raspberry pastries. I'd been stress eating since my father became sick, often making myself throw up afterward.

From his bed, my father called out my name. I went to him.

"Do you want to have breakfast together?" he asked.

"No, thanks, I already ate. Dad, do you want me to stay home with you, or can I go see a movie with some friends?"

I'd begun to feel guilty if I didn't spend time with him on the weekends.

"Go on with your friends. There is no reason why you should have to stay in the house all day."

I kissed him goodbye. He looked so sweet, like a child; all his defenses were down.

A few hours later, while I was in a movie theater laughing at Christopher Guest's *Best in Show*, my father's lung was collapsing, he was screaming my mother's name, and my ten-year-old brother was calling 9-1-1. My mother was with him the moment he died, his face contorted in terror, then lifeless. I am grateful I was not present to witness this, as I'm sure it would have caused me nightmares for many years. My mother never talks about whether or not she has nightmares, and I never ask.

When the paramedics lifted my father's body up onto the gurney, my brother placed a small gold *World's Greatest Dad* trophy on the center of his chest, a gift from us the Father's Day prior. Then the paramedics zipped up the body bag, rolled him out the door, up the ramp into the van, and then he was gone.

I was in the car with my friends on the way back to my house when I turned on my cell phone to see I had several missed calls with messages from my mother. My friend Melissa was driving.

"My dad's dead," I said.

"What? How do you know?" said Melissa. "You're probably just jumping to conclusions." But she said it to the windshield, her hands wrapped tightly around the steering wheel. When we got to my house, I asked her and John to please wait outside. I went in, and my mother, looking awfully pale, grabbed my hand and pulled me toward my bedroom past her best friend, who was seated at our kitchen table. She put her hand on my shoulder and looked at the wall behind me. She seemed shell-shocked.

"Dad passed away today. His lung collapsed. The ambulance—"

I wasn't listening anymore. I couldn't process the information. It's like what I hear happens when people have limbs bit off by sharks; the shock is so great they don't feel a thing. I remember literally feeling numbness in my body. I ran back outside where my friends were waiting and tried to force myself to cry. That's what I thought I was supposed to do. With all my might, I strained to push out tears, to give birth to them. They were stuck, inaccessible; my eyes had never been drier. I squeezed Melissa to me. I wanted to prolong this squeezing for as long as possible, didn't want to go back into that house, didn't want to go into my father's room and see his oxygen tank, his empty bed.

Tiffany had been at a track meet in northern California when my father died. She was due back on Sunday evening. My mom had called her coach to tell him what had happened, and together they agreed it would be best not to tell Tiffany, and let her run her races. She would find out when she got home. Tiffany never got over the fact that he had been dead for two days without her knowing.

Two nights later when the track van pulled up in front of our house, I sat in the living room by the window and watched my mom speak to the coach in the driver's seat. She was asking him to wait for a minute while my mom brought my sister inside to tell her in case, like me, she wanted to run back out to hug her friends. She brought her into her room and delivered the news. A few minutes later, my mom emerged and went outside to tell the coach that my sister wouldn't be coming back out. Tiffany stayed in her room with the door closed for several hours.

Later that night, after my mom and brother had gone to sleep, I went into the kitchen for some water. I heard the song "Tears in Heaven" playing softly from my father's office. I peeked my head in to see my sister sitting at his desk and crying hard with her whole body. She was looking at a picture of herself sleeping on his shoulder as a toddler. I laid my hand on her back.

"Do you want to go for a walk?"

"Okay," she said and fell into me, squeezing my waist. Tiffany and I hadn't been particularly close as teenagers, and rarely showed each other physical affection. We went out into the dark and walked silently. I listened to her cry. At the edge of our neighborhood, there was a bench overlooking a canyon. We sat down while she continued to cry softly. I put my arm around her. It was a clear temperate San Diego night; the stars were bright and piercing, the neighborhood silent. We sat for a while, breathing, her final tears leaking out, until she stood up and I followed suit. We walked back to our house and each went into our bedrooms. Tiffany and I hadn't spoken a single word the entire time, but I had never felt so close to her.

For his funeral, I made a program on a sheet of eight-and-a-half by eleven-inch paper folded horizontally that I photocopied for the guests. On the front, I glued the surgeon general's warning from a cigarette box: *Smoking Causes Lung Cancer, Heart Disease, Emphysema, And May Complicate Pregnancy.* On the top inside page, I pasted the lyrics from two of his favorite songs, "Radar Love" by Golden Earring and "All Along the Watchtower" by Bob Dylan. On the bottom page, I handwrote a poem I had written for him, and on the back cover, I handwrote five things he said to me that stuck in my mind: *Be careful. Don't forget to take your key. Call when you know what time you'll be home. I love you. Let's go for a walk.* I handed the program to guests as they arrived.

It was a gray day and looked like it was going to rain. Everyone stood while my family and I sat beside the casket. I stared into the grave as the rabbi spoke. I didn't cry during the service, feeling more ponderous than grief-stricken. When the rabbi finished, he called upon our family to each say a few words if we so desired. My mom and sister declined. My brother and I stood. In his little voice, my brother said, "I loved my dad. I liked playing baseball with him and stuff. I'm going to miss him." Then he sat down, and I stepped up and read my poem. Rain clouds gathered overhead, and a breeze picked up. Then the casket was lowered, and everyone took a turn dumping a shovel's worth of dirt onto the grave, as is the custom in Judaism. It started raining halfway through, but we all just stood there for a while, watching the dirt turn to mud.

My siblings and I looked to my mother for clues about how to proceed. "Life goes on," she told us, so we followed her lead. There was work to be done, no time to indulge in self-pity. During that time, I never saw her cry but wondered what went on inside her upon falling asleep at night. I was always too nervous to ask.

Time didn't stop. When I went back to school after taking a week off, I had piles of homework and tests to make up. It seemed completely absurd to me that the rest of the world just kept going as if nothing were different. Everything *was* different.

In the evenings, my family continued to sit around the dinner table, accounting for our days.

"I scored a goal at soccer practice," Austin said, chomping a fish stick.

"That's nice," said my mom. "And how was your day?" she asked Tiffany.

"Fine," she said, peeling the breading off her fish.

"And you?" my mom asked me.

"Also fine."

No heavy breathing, no coughing, no muttering. No Dad.

Once I woke up in the middle of the night to go to the bathroom, expecting to see my father sitting in his chair in the living room. At first I was startled to find it empty; then consciousness seeped back in and brought reality into focus. I sat down in his chair in the dark and dug my fingers into the armrests until my knuckles were white. I became hypnotized by the sound of my own breathing. So reliable: one breath, then another, then another, then—

I look at the sky every day.
When the earth's ceiling looks particularly blue
And the sun is shining particularly bright
I think I can see your eyes
The hazel and the white
They don't look so tired
There are no tubes in your nose
Your feet are not swollen
And you're wiggling your toes
Because life is so beautiful
Beautiful every day
And every day upon waking
I look at the sky
Sun in my eyes
Earth's ceiling so blue
Your particular smile is shining right through

What Is Language?

After my father died, I transferred all my hot grief energy into taking life by storm; I felt like I was on fire, fearless and unstoppable. Concretely aware for the first time that life was fragile and finite, I wanted to make mine as dynamic as possible. I was cast as the lead in the next high school play. I competed and won prizes in state-wide monologue, scene, and improvisation competitions. I was editor-in-chief of my school's literary magazine. In the spring, I was accepted to NYU's Tisch School of the Arts for Acting. I spoke at my high school commencement ceremony, urging my classmates to define success for themselves and to strive for it. The following fall, I moved to New York City to start college.

In my first two years studying at the Stella Adler Conservatory, I discovered my vast range of physical, vocal, and emotional expression. I couldn't believe this all lay within me before without my knowing. Movement classes had me stretching, dancing, rolling on the floor, rolling over others, massaging others, being massaged, absorbing the connection between breath and movement. Voice classes taught me that generating powerful, resonant vocal sound was a full-body endeavor. I practiced by lying on the floor, inhaling deeply into the space below my navel, uniting my breath with my voice, relaxing my face and body, opening my mouth and expelling voice at the ceiling in a slow, steady stream. Exercises with the muscles of my lips, face, and tongue taught me to fully experience the formation of vowels and consonants. The mechanics of speaking and moving, basic things I did all the time, began to enrapture me.

My classmates and teachers were all fiercely creative and talented, inspiring me beyond belief. I became fearless on stage, amazed at how I could conjure any emotion and really experience it if I connected deeply with the imagined reality of the scene. I could do anything: scream, cry, dance, flail, strip, make out. I loved pushing myself to extremes and receiving wildly positive feedback. I had never felt so alive and free.

To top it off, I had just moved from San Diego to New York City and was swiftly seduced by the romance of it all. My floor mates were all artists looking to get their crazy on. Living in Greenwich Village, there were tons of bars that didn't card, which was ridiculously exciting. On weekend nights, we frequented an underground jazz bar on MacDougal Street called Café Creole, where we stayed up all night drinking Long Island iced teas, talking about art and philosophy, and making each other laugh insanely. We stumbled home from bars in the wee hours, flouncing through the empty city streets, dancing, singing, laughing, chatting, and smoking joints. As we approached our dormitory, the black sky would be transitioning to faint blue, exposing the first traces of morning. A pale gold enveloped the surrounding buildings as we slipped through the front door.

During the second week of school, two planes crashed into the World Trade Center, and school was cancelled for a week. My dorm was on Fifth Avenue and Tenth Street, in the area blocked off below Fourteenth. For most of the week, my floor mates and I sat together in the hallway in shock, not knowing what else to do, unable to process the magnitude of what had happened just a few miles south of our new home. Sitting on that ratty green carpet under the fluorescent lights for so many hours, we got to know each other's intimate histories pretty quickly. But eventually we ran out of things to say, so we went back into our rooms and watched movie after movie, trying to freeze our thoughts, going stir-crazy. Finally one night, this guy John hauled a mini trampoline out into the hallway and knocked on all our doors, calling out, "Come on, guys, let's go outside." We turned off our TVs and followed him. A girl brought sidewalk chalk. When we got outside, the streets and sidewalks were deserted, and a smell of burnt steel and flesh wafted up Fifth Avenue. The few people out held their shirts over their noses to block the odor. We walked to the corner of Mac-Dougal and West 3rd Street, where we jumped on the trampoline and drew on the asphalt. We sang songs and joked around for the first time in nearly a week.

But the relief was short-lived. For the next couple of days, I really didn't know what to do with myself and almost felt the impulse to start scratching at the walls. When classes finally started up again, I was so grateful for the structure they provided. Theater became an even stronger emotional outlet for me; I couldn't imagine my life without it.

My second year, I formed my own improv comedy troupe with a friend and began performing in a weekly variety show at a small performance space/bar in the East Village. I developed a roster of characters, including a drunk homeless woman from the eighties, an interpretive dancer who only performed to soundtracks from Disney movies, and a deranged woman who wrote passionate nonsensical songs to her lost love, accompanying herself on guitar. My co-improv troupe founder and I created an act called *Punchy and Pinchy,* a male/female duo dressed in mouse costumes that bantered about taboo subjects like porn, guns, and STDs. I loved creating my own performance material, the more absurd, the better. I was obsessed with Gilda Radner. My ambitions were erupting; one of my goals quickly became writing and performing for *Saturday Night Live.*

Also in my second year, I linked up with my friend Adam from Stella Adler who was interested in making his own performance work as well. We each wrote a play in the absurdist theater genre and joined them with *The Bald Soprano* by Eugene Ionesco for an evening of Absurdist Theater in a black box at Stella Adler. It garnered an enthusiastic response, and I was elated. Adam and I started fantasizing about the company we would have together when we graduated.

Toward the end of my second year, I applied to a five-week summer program through NYU studying *Commedia Del Arte* in Florence, Italy, and was accepted. I also auditioned for a spot in the Experimental Theatre Wing's Transfer Track, which was highly competitive, and I got in. Then, at the end of my sophomore year as I was preparing to go to Italy, I received a letter informing me that I had enough credits to graduate in three years because of the Advanced Placement and community college credits with which I'd entered. While the option remained to stay in school a fourth year, it didn't make any sense to pay the high tuition for a year I didn't need for my degree. I was shocked. Theater school had become such an enthralling bubble; I had no idea how to approach life in the outside world and was overcome with gnawing apprehension, then resolved to shove these feelings aside and enjoy the present as much as possible.

But ultimately the second semester of that third year arrived, and with impending graduation, I became paralyzed by fear of the unknown, and my castle of ambition began to crumble. Losing the structure and built-in community of school seemed catastrophic. How the hell was I going to make a living as a theater artist? The profession was not stable, and I didn't know what I was supposed to do for steady income. I didn't invest all that time, money, and passion just to graduate and start doing some random job that I hated. Also, I had been moving at such an accelerated speed for so long, I was exhausted. I didn't have the energy to suddenly start making all these complicated decisions on my own. Fear, grief, and anxiety devoured me, making it impossible to think clearly or rationally. Instead of making plans or getting counseling to assist with the transition, I completely deflated and drew inward. I grew resentful of my roommates, who were still in party mode, drinking and playing music all night in our dumpy East Village apartment.

The more I withdrew, the more I resented performing, being forced to stand in front of people and expose myself when I wanted to curl up in my closet under a pile of clothes. Whenever I did get up in class to perform, I either felt vacant or raw; I mouthed the words of the scene, monologue, or song feeling like I had left my body, or I got up there and wanted to cry the whole time. As for improv, the members of my troupe had stopped making improv their priority, as they were getting involved in productions, and I was tired of trying to reel them back in, so we quietly disbanded. It was fine with me; I wasn't feeling funny anyway. My friends and roommates were all engrossed in their own projects and lives, so they didn't particularly notice. When I wasn't in class, I was usually in bed.

My mother suggested I apply to graduate school. Though I didn't have strong aspirations to go, I had no other ideas. I applied to NYU for playwriting and The New School for creative writing, then spent the rest of the semester sinking into a pit of lethargy and apathy. My mom, brother, and sister flew to New York for my graduation ceremony, but I didn't even want to go, didn't feel that my being released into the world was really something to celebrate.

Shortly after graduating, The New School accepted me into the creative nonfiction program. I would be a graduate student at the age of twenty-one, though I wasn't completely convinced it was the right decision. My mom was ecstatic; I wished I could have been.

I went home to San Diego for the summer, and when I returned to New York in the fall, I felt recharged, ready for a new beginning. The idea of earning a master's degree at the age of twenty-three began to excite me; I was the youngest person in the program. My ambitions re-accelerated; I landed an internship at Performance Space 122 and started working on a puppet dance piece at the La Mama Experimental Theater on top of my classes and work for the writing program. I was maniacally addicted to creative projects; they gave me a purpose. Experience had taught me that when I lost that purpose, I lost myself.

The New School classes were two nights a week, and my classmates and I always went out to a bar afterward, where we drank whiskey in the dark and talked romantically about writing until the room started to spin. I connected especially well with three men and one woman; they became my go-to clique. I drank my fair share of liquor as an undergraduate, but in writing school, drinking made me feel particularly whimsical. I started drinking more and more, to the point where I was passing out in bars. I'd wake up in my dorm room the next morning in my clothes and shoes, not remembering how I got there. My friends switched off taking me home in cabs and eventually began scolding me to clean up my act.

I had a brief fling with one of the three men, though we never actually had sex. His name was Michael and he was in the fiction program, twelve years my senior. Michael was the quintessential writer type: thin, pale, and melancholic, with dark hair and black-rimmed glasses, lots of button-down shirts. I found the idea of him very attractive. He lived alone in a studio apartment near Gramercy Park.

One night, I pounded three vodka martinis at a bar by myself and was feeling lonely, so I trekked to his apartment at 1:30 a.m., buzzed, and woke him. He let me up, opening his door wearing a T-shirt and boxer shorts, rubbing the sleep from his eyes.

"I'm sorry for coming so late. But...can I stay with you? I'm lonely."

"You're drunk," he said, without blinking.

"Yeah, well…" I moved to hug him and tripped over my feet. I regained my balance and looped my arms tightly around his torso. I like to feel you breathe. *I like to get the knots out of your back. I like that you like my fingers, that you want more of them.*

He bent his elbows back, reached behind himself, and peeled my wrists off his body.

"Amanda, you're drunk," he repeated. "I think you should go home."

I stared at him for a long time, trying to stomach the rejection.

"Call me when you get there."

I stared at him a moment longer, then closed my eyes, replaying our dialogue from the night before.

"Do you mind if I pull your hair?" he said.

"No."

"Do you like it?"

"Yes."

"You don't have to say you like something if you don't."

"But I do."

"You're beautiful, you know."

"You're beautiful, too," I said.

"Beautiful on the inside."

I turned, flung open the door, and headed out into the hallway. He stood in the doorway, watching me while I waited for the elevator. After an eternity, it finally arrived.

"Call me when you get home," he repeated.

I didn't say anything as the door slid closed. I called him when I got home, but I never went to his apartment again.

In December, when the internship, show, and semester ended, I went home to San Diego for winter break. Going home always disoriented me now that my life existed in such a different context; it felt simultaneously foreign and familiar. It was a kind of psychological trick; just when I would be adjusting to the comfort of being with my family, it was time to leave again. This time when I returned to the city for the new semester, I had significantly less drive and felt burnt out. I got a job doing administrative work two days a week for a performance space and attended the writing classes two nights a week. But it was not enough structure. I didn't know how to fill these giant days I had all to myself. They stretched so long, endless white spaces. It started taking me longer and longer to get out of bed in the morning. Often I woke up in tears, dreading the stress of having to deal with all this time. The more time I had, the less motivated I was to do my schoolwork. I began to doubt my place in graduate school, having lost my inspiration to write and lacking the desire to read the assigned books.

I started turning in streams of gibberish for writing workshop: *"Food. Coffee. Fat. Body. Ow, my neck. What is. Dark! Cold! Who am I? (Am who)."* Before class one night, my teacher pulled me into his office and said, "It's going to be very difficult for us to discuss your piece. I'd like to know what your goals are for this program." I shrugged my shoulders; I didn't know what my goals were for anything.

Mid-February: the thick of winter. The snow fell lightly on the suits scurrying to their corporate cubicles with coffee in hand. The sky was a pale blue-gray. I sat on the interior window ledge of my New School dormitory in the financial district, four floors up on the corner of William Street and Maiden Lane. From there, I watched the stream of coats accumulate thin sheets of white. The crisp cold breath of outside was leaking in through the air conditioning vent just below the window.

Seated cross-legged, sweatpants, socked feet, sweatshirt hood over my head, I began to study the ball of lint in my hand, which I'd extracted from the dryer and pressed between my fingers as I climbed the stairs to my room: Gray. Wrapped in hair. Shades of blue and purple, glittering in the sunlight. Soft, like a tuft of lamb's wool. Not for eating. No smell. I held it to my ear and rubbed my thumb against it ever so gently, to ensure that the lint ball didn't fall apart, and listened to sounds reminiscent of erasers rubbing together. I continued to roll it around between my fingers; it began to disintegrate.

I hugged my knees to my chest, closed my eyes, and let the cold air pour across my face while I questioned who and what I was. I considered the basic facts. I was a female human byproduct of a sperm and an egg. After implanting in the uterus, swishing around in water and developing all my human parts, I was birthed. Breathed oxygen. Ate. Shat. Learned to crawl. Learned to talk. Learned to walk around. But what the hell was my purpose?

I lived in the common room. It was terrible; my two roommates had to walk through my room to get to the bathroom or the door to the outside. That was what I got for applying for the cheapest housing. As I lay in bed, cursing my consciousness, I dreaded the moment one of them would open her door and enter my space. I heard an alarm go off in the other room, and my heart started pounding. I didn't want to see anyone or have to talk; I just wanted to be left in peace. Any minute, I would hear the jarring sound of that knob turning and feet pattering across the hard wood floor. My chest and stomach tightened up. I rubbed my forehead and temples in anticipation.

"Good morning," one of the girls would say.

"Good morning," I'd answer.

And that would be it. There was not much to say to each other, never had been. Suddenly she emerged, just as I'd predicted. I held my breath. She didn't say anything as she walked past me and into the bathroom. I was relieved. After several minutes, she came back out and asked me, "Do you think you could clean the bathroom today?"

I seized up and cleared my throat. "Sure," I said, and rolled over to face the wall.

I took up walking aimlessly through the streets of Lower Manhattan, like an automaton. The street sounds disconnected from their sources, becoming meaningless chaotic noise. People screamed into their cell phones, cabs honked, tires screeched. Homeless people jingled cups for change, jackhammers pounded. The sights also blurred together. Bodies swarmed in all directions, scrambling in and out of buildings, flooding sidewalks, morphing into dual-gendered, multi-headed creatures. The wind ripped through me, tall buildings blocked the sun. I walked and walked. Shrinking.

Then, after business hours, the financial district turned into a ghost town. I walked through the maze of empty, windy streets for hours, with no destination, simply to avoid having to see my room-

mates and be in a position where I might have to speak to someone. I pattered down narrow twisted alleys, surrounded by vacant
corporate buildings scraping the sky. The World Trade Center hole.
One bodega, two bodega, three bodega, four. My feet seemed to
move by themselves. I'd been down that street already. That one,
too. No matter. I was not headed anywhere as I moved through the
space, ghost-like.

Occasionally I caught glimpses of myself in store windows.
Who was that person? Me? Could other people see me? I started to
find it strange that I couldn't see my face without a reflective surface, didn't know what it looked like to the rest of the world. Of
course it would have made no sense for me to be able to see my
face all the time; that was impossible. However, if I couldn't see it,
how did I know it was there? Just the torso, legs, forearms, and
hands dangling from my elbow. But the face? The head? I would
stare at myself in the window for a long time. Into my eyes. At my
pores. Stare at my face and touch its reflection. Then touch my
actual face again. I felt hollow.

I often sat alone in Barnes and Noble with my assigned reading. I
stared at the pages of my books, not actually absorbing any of the
words, just looking at them as symbols. I started thinking about the
process of reading and writing, transmitting thoughts from one
brain to another via words on a page. Then I considered language
and communication as a phenomenon unto itself: How bizarre it
was that all of reality was a language construct. What was language,
really? How could we take it for granted?

My innocent analysis transitioned quickly into full-blown obsession. Every sentence I spoke lingered; I deconstructed it in my
head long after its utterance, picking it apart word by word, fixating
on each syllable and sound, and how the words carried individual
and collective meaning. My voice began to feel frightfully foreign
when it slipped out of my lips and into the air. This made socializing nearly impossible. While I was maniacally examining the last

thing I said, the other person would be speaking. Then I'd shift my
attention to that person's words and shirked the task of decipher-
ing the whole exchange; the meaning of the conversation was soon
nullified, and I would find a reason to slink away.

2/5/05

I am made of matter. I take up space. All my matter joins together to coagu-
late into this viscous mass that is ME, and a part of ME is this brain be-
tween my ears, behind my eyes.
What would happen if I could break through this word barrier?
What realm would I enter into?
What would happen if I exploded the dictionary?
Would it break the sound barrier?
What is the correlation between words and sound, anyway?
E-v-e-r-y-t-h-i-n-g i-s r-e-l-a-t-e-d.
All   things   are   one.

Sam and I were lying on the twin mattress in his dorm room, his
arms wrapped around me while we listened to "The Sounds of Silence" by Simon and Garfunkel. I closed my eyes and thought of my
father, then opened them and refocused on Sam. He was another of
the three men in my social group, six foot two, wide-set, a big soft
teddy bear with blue eyes and a full head of fluffy sandy-blond hair.
Sam had been making romantic overtures toward me since the day
we met. However, I was not attracted to him and told him repeatedly
that I just wanted to be his friend. Then, one night in a bar after the
Michael incident, I had pounded two whiskeys and, filled with romantic longing, I kissed him and we started seeing each other.

   "Don't you think it's bizarre that our entire reality is a language construct?" I asked. "I can't seem to wrap my head around
it. What *is* language?"

   "That question is not useful to either one of us. Remember,
Wittgenstein said we expunge the sentences that don't get us any further. I think the real question you mean to ask is, 'What is sandwich'?"

Sam's presence soothed me. I came to him in states of panic, brain spinning, and I poured my thoughts out. He listened without judgment and gave me tight generous hugs. The longer I spent in his company, the more at ease I began to feel. The panic slowly dissipated, and there were long stretches of time when these thoughts did not attack me. He was the only person with whom I could comfortably spend my time.

I climbed on top of him and kissed him on the mouth. He kissed me back, eagerly, tenderly.

"You know, I feel so lucky to have you here," he said.

"No, I feel lucky."

"No, I do."

"No, I do."

"*Ich liebe dich*," he said, German for "I love you." "There's some language for you."

He kissed the back of my hand. I licked and bit his ear. He shivered and moaned with pleasure. For a flash, I felt less like a ghost. My breasts took shape under his hands. His lips and tongue created my neck and face. Two sets of legs and feet—his, mine.

2/18/05

Eyewitness Report

"I saw the girl," he said. "She was wearing a green wool sweater. I saw her wearing it. She saw me. I asked her to dance with me. She said yes. We drank whiskey and danced the night away. At the end of the night I kissed her. She came home with me. I can vouch that there is a body under that sweater."

Back in my dorm room, I woke up angry. What the hell was I doing awake? Why was I waking up again? What was there to do? How was I capable of thinking these thoughts in the first place? My head started to spin, and it hadn't even left the pillow.

2/20/05

Head	*Face*	*Eyes*
Ears	*Lips*	*Liver*

And all the other human parts

This obsession with voice and words spiraled into obsession with the terms of my own existence. How was it that I had feeling in this body that I lived in? What was pleasure? What was pain? Mirrors and recognition in the eyes of others seemed to confirm that I was a living, breathing entity. When I looked down, I could see my body extending to the floor in the space below my neck. I could feel the winter wind whip through me as I rounded corners of New York City streets. My name was on class lists, on a door to an apartment, on two mailboxes; it would be impossible not to deduce that I was a living, breathing human creature. But somehow, I wasn't fully convinced. I craved a break from thinking and speaking.

I started seeing a school therapist. I sat in her office and babbled for thirty to forty-five minutes. She had no idea what I was talking about. It was more harmful than helpful to be confronted by her glazed stare.

"I just want to feel like a whole person all day," was one of the things I told her.

"Okay."

"Does that make any sense?"

"Yes, it does. It's just hard for me to understand where you're coming from because it doesn't seem like you necessarily know where you're coming from."

"I know, it's frustrating, isn't it?"

"Tell me a little about your family. What was it like growing up?"

"Okay." I relayed details about my family and what it was like growing up, in perfect English sentences.

"And have you ever had thoughts about suicide?"

"Of course, who hasn't?"

"But you've never attempted to commit suicide?"

"No, though I used to scratch at my wrists with plastic razors when I was twelve and thirteen." I looked down at my lap, feeling like an idiot for admitting this.

The therapist jotted something down in her notebook.

"And any drugs?"

"I mean, some pot from time to time. But not lately."

"Anything else?"

"No."

I was lying. I'd taken acid in tenth grade with a friend I met in eating disorder group therapy. But this was a non sequitur that would be of little to no use to this woman trying to make sense of the blabbering fool in her office.

"And it says here in your counseling history that you were seen for anorexia?"

"Yes."

"For how long?"

"About two years."

"And can you tell me a little bit about what that was like?"

I slumped in my chair and entered a staring contest with the rug. It needed to be washed. Its edges were frayed. I looked up at the woman across from me as she pushed her red-rimmed glasses up her nose and took a sip of water. Her right leg was crossed over her left, foot bouncing slightly. I looked back at the rug.

I relayed details about being hospitalized for anorexia at age fourteen, squirming in my seat.

"So why did you decide to come to therapy this time around?"

"I don't know...to put my voice in this room, to see what words decided to bounce off my tongue into your ears."

"I see."

She scribbled notes onto her pad. I listened to the sound of the clock ticking.

Stiff-necked, arms like crowbars. Dragging protesting body from bodega to bodega, swallowing pieces of pastry, barely chewed. I bought a pack of cookie dough. Back at the dorm, I plopped myself down in the stairwell. Tore open a corner, threw my head back, and squeezed over half the package down my throat. A person in a coat rushed past me down the stairs, and a scampering foot slammed into my leg. I whipped myself up violently and stomped back to my room, heading straight for the toilet, dough in hand. I dropped the dough in my apartment doorway. Roommates not home.

Panting in bathroom. I leaned over the toilet bowl and shoved the tops of my fingers into my guts. Instant vomiting. Gassy chunks were forced back up through my throat, sometimes got stuck. I lifted my head up and looked in the mirror: My face was pink and puffy, eyes bloodshot. Gagging on dough, my body heaved. Taste in my mouth of partially digested sugar butter soaked in stomach acid. I choked. I spit. I leaned over the toilet again and jammed my fists hard into my stomach. Cursed at myself.

The toilet bowl was a mix of drippy oozy mucous-coated dough blobs; there were some chunks of carrot from earlier in the day. I scream-moaned through clenched teeth. Acid burned my throat. I flushed the toilet and bit the top of my bicep hard, leaving teeth clenched there for as long as thirty seconds. Released my grip. Deep purple grooves. Slammed my forearms into the wall, fists still gripped, ripped my clothes off, got in the shower. Made sure the water was scalding hot. Hands on my stomach. Bathroom hot boxed with steam. Mirror completed clouded over. I got out of the shower and plopped down on the cold bathroom tiled floor, naked and soaking wet. Stood up. Flushed. Turned off the water. Toweled dry. Out into my room to dress and hit the icy dark and deserted streets of the financial district to return to aimless wandering, panicked and crazed. Time for another jaunt across the Brooklyn Bridge. Maybe I'd hit up a bar for a couple shots of whiskey on the way. See if anyone had any funny stories to tell.

3/8/05

These letters all fit together to form words which, when laced together with thought, specificity, and punctuation, form sentences. String these sentences together, and you have paragraphs. And when all this passes through your eye into your brain, you have meaning.

"I'll be there in forty-five minutes. I'll sing my way there," I said to Sam…in words…two complete sentences.

"I'll wait for you."

(A female form passes through the door. The door closes.)

Here I go, out into the rain.

It felt good to have Sam rubbing up against me, reminding me of my body, that it could still respond to stimulation. Our hips ground into each other, breaths sped up until they were syncopated. But I didn't want to have sex with him; I was irrationally terrified of becoming pregnant. If there was an ejaculation within ten feet of me, I was convinced I would need an abortion.

"I think we should cool our jets," I told him. That was a weird thing to say. Jets… spelled J-E-T-S. I sounded it out in my head: *j-e-e-e-t-t-s-s-s*. Did I just say that?

"I can get a condom," he said. *Condom, condom, condom, condom*…when repeated over and over, the word lost all meaning.

"No, I don't want to." *O I o a o*: That was the sentence without consonants.

In the midst of this linguistic analysis, I was giving him a hand job, not paying enough attention, and then he came. There was no actual penetration; nevertheless, I was terrified. I should have rolled off him before that stuff came squirting out.

I froze up. "I have to go home," I said.

"Everything is fine; nothing happened. What's the matter?"

I dressed quickly, gave him a pat-on-the-back hug, and sped through the common room where six of his roommates (they lived in an eleven-person suite) were drinking beer and watching *Major League*. He ran after me into the hall. He looked concerned.

"Can I walk you to the subway?" he asked.

"No, thanks," I said, "I'd rather be alone. Good night." I gave him a fast hug. We parted at the elevator.

I muttered the words, "Good night, good night," to myself in the elevator, through the lobby, out to the street, on the walk to the subway. "Good night, good night. *Oo i. Gd nt*."

Night time.

Financial district.

Bodega.

"I'll have a cookie, please," I said, startled by the sound of my own voice as usual.

Cookie please, cookie please, cookie please. Please. Please. Pleeeeeeaaaasssssseee. P L E A S E.

"That will be one dollar."

Daaaaawwwwwlllllirrrrrrrrrrrrrrr.

Clip. Clop. Clip. Clop. The sound of my feet on the ground. Up down, up down. Rhythmic footsteps.

I clip-clopped to the Brooklyn Bridge.

Standing on the bridge, looking out over the Manhattan skyline, I bit the inside of my cheek until it bled in an effort to taste myself. What a panorama.

I was a part of that place, I was a human being. I had warm blood pumping through my veins. I could speak. I could sing. That night, I was singing out over the traffic, canoodling my voice into its swishhhh.

It started as a hum. Then it escalated slowly until it reached CRESCENDO. I was singing George Harrison's "All Things Must Pass."

I called my voice mailbox and left a message for myself, singing. Then I called my messages and listened to my voice in awe.

Inside my brain there were rainbows of words, even if they did sometimes get lost in the wind when they flew off my tongue, through my teeth and into the air. I climbed up above the water onto the bridge's ledge, just to test my balance.

Vodka martini binge. East 20th Street between Sixth and Seventh Avenue. Two a.m. I'd gone to the bar with Sam and was wasted. Out on the street, I started crying, then wailing. He'd seen me cry before; he was patient beyond belief.

"Why are you with me?" I asked him.

"I love you."

"Why?"

"I just do."

I cried harder. Then I hurled my body onto the pavement.

"Leave me here!" I screamed. "Please, just leave me here!"

"Get out of the street!" he shouted, tears running down his face. "I'm not going to leave you here!"

He pulled me by the arm, hailed a cab, and pushed me into it, getting in next to me. "William Street and Maiden Lane," he said.

Back in my dorm room, I pounded the floor, crying ferociously.

"What can I do? What can I do?" he kept asking.

"Nothing," I grunted, "Go away. Wait, I'm sorry. Thank you."

4/28/05

Words on a page

Words on a page

Words on a page

W-o-r-d-s o-n a p**a**g**e**

w

                                    o

r

                               d

sssssssssssssssssssssssssssssssssssssssssssssssssssssssssssss

& @ ! $ ^ _ +)

3:17 p.m. When I looked in the mirror and saw my face, I realized I was still here.

3:31 p.m. Still here. So it seems.

3:35 p.m. Still here. So it seems.

3:41 p.m. Still here. So it seems.

Word after word after word after word after word after word after word after word

Afterward.

Forward.

Backward.

Words that start with "B":
betwixt, befuddled, bemused, bereft, beer, big, bunny, blintzes, Byzantine, Bermuda, Beirut, bojangles, Boston, bow, bunt, bundt cake, boring, basket, bungalow, Beckett

Words that start with "S":
sorry, sin, science, Sartre, Susan, sand, sandbox, sandpaper, San Diego, sock, soccer, suck, suck-it, soap

INTERJECTION:
When Sam asked me, "So, what do you want to do tonight?"
    And my response was, "I don't know what I'm doing with my life,"
    He scolded me disparagingly, "This is not your life; this is one night."

RETURN TO WORD THOUGHTS:
If I could stop thinking about language for one second, I would...
c l i m b - m o u n t - e v e r e s t
s i n g - t h e - s t a r - s p a n g l e d - b a n n e r
in the shower
without thinking about the way "the rocket's red glare" is spelled and spaced out on a page, the way the words sound when they roll off my tongue and bounce off the bathroom wall, what the words mean, what they are, why they are.

I think all this talk about words is making numbers jealous.

5   29   14   18   76

198,376,451, 675, 548, 321, 678, 904

+ / - divided by X the square root of

? ? ? ? ?

p l a i n   t e x t

4:15 p.m.- Still here. So it seems.

In his own words
In her own words

In simple words
Beyond words

Words pale when I try to express my gratitude for simply existing; that is, assuming I do.

I tried a different therapist:

"You are here," she said. "I promise. Those are your legs. These are your hands. Those are your eyes. That is your mouth. These are your ears. Between them is your brain."

   Whose voice?
   Whose hands?
   Whose feet?
   Mine.
   Belonging to me.
   To the human being that she claims I am.
   At the end of the semester, I left New York and moved back in with my mother in San Diego.

5/11/05
Dear Dad,

   So what do you think about the current state of your oldest daughter? Any advice?

If so, please transport it to her via dream.

Remember how it didn't always used to be like this? Remember when she used to know she was a person?

With love from your ghost of a live daughter

(Who's, ironically enough, writing a letter to a ghost)

I miss you

Home

When I first returned home, my mother was angry. She made me feel like a failure, a huge disappointment. How could I just drop out of the program? Why couldn't I have pulled it together? So she did what she always does, everything in her power to solve the problem through practical measures; she immediately steered me to a psychiatrist and psychotherapist.

My psychiatrist seemed entirely apathetic. He was a small man, balding with some gray hair and a gray beard. I sat with him in his office while he looked through me. None of my symptoms seemed to register with him.

"It sounds a little schizophrenic," he said dismissively, though I was never officially diagnosed with schizophrenia. (Terms like depersonalization, detachment, panic disorder, and depression were also tossed around.) Nevertheless, he prescribed Abilify, an antipsychotic used to treat depression, schizophrenia, and mania, which didn't help but rather caused stiffness in my joints to the point that I couldn't bend my wrists or fingers. Then I tried Geodon, another antipsychotic for schizophrenia and bipolar mania. That gave me insomnia, the worst possible side effect, seeing as I wanted to avoid consciousness for as long as possible. So I stopped taking that, too.

My therapist also seemed unfeeling. As if nothing I said resonated with her in any way, she offered no suggestions. Every time I went in, I had no new information to divulge, so I would sit and stare at her. She made agonizing attempts to prod me, attempting to fill the forty-five-minute sessions. Eventually, after sitting and

staring at her for several months without a change, she called in my
mother and me to say she didn't know how to help me, that I
should try someone else. My mother felt helpless and panicked. I
had a good education. I was intelligent. She wondered what she did
wrong and worried that I would never snap out of it. She took me
to a neurologist to have an MRI brain scan; maybe there was something fundamentally wrong with my brain. The MRI results were
normal.

I hid under the covers and drugged myself with television for
the majority of my conscious hours, particularly *E! True Hollywood
Stories* and *Roseanne*. (I actually got so addicted to *Roseanne* that I
purchased the whole series from Amazon.) However, television
continued to pose a problem as I fixated on the words being spoken by the TV characters, wondering how they meant anything. I
stayed mostly in my mother's bed or on the couch with a blanket
and a pillow. "Why don't you take a break from television and read
a book," she suggested. "No," I replied, horrified, "I can't. I can't
read anymore." If I opened a page of text, I stared at the black-on-
white symbols, my eyes refusing to travel across them. Looking at
words hyped up my awareness of language and exacerbated my
anxiety; reading was the last activity I needed. I ate mechanically,
never exercised, and gained twenty-five pounds. Every social encounter with a person who was not in my immediate family elicited
intense terror and panic, even people who were my close friends or
who had known me for years.

One day, after a couple of months like this, my mother flicked
off the television, tore off my covers, and told me I had to get a
job. I grudgingly started working at Round Table Pizza down the
street. It made me anxious to have to be around people this long.
Any time anyone would talk to me, I'd be flooded by waves of
nerves. I thought that when I spoke people couldn't understand
me, though of course they always could. We spoke the same language. But it never felt like it was I who was speaking. I didn't feel
like myself at all.

All my life's possessions were contained in my bedroom in my mother's house: photo albums, books, journals, CDs, keepsakes, clothing, all the furniture I had painted as a teenager. I couldn't conceive that these were my things. They seemed to belong to somebody else. I would be in my room studying these items for hours, especially the photo albums. I studied the photographs of me enjoying myself, smiling, at a party with friends, in a play. Who was that? Was I really a person with a past? Similarly, I'd spend hours staring at my reflection in the mirror, studying my face: my eyes, the lines on my forehead, the lines at the sides of my eyes when I squinted. I opened and closed my mouth. I considered I might be dead.

I thought about how strange it was that there was feeling in my body. I lay on the floor, bending, stretching, and wiggling my hands and feet, fingers and toes. My body existed in the same dimension as the floor. Why couldn't I feel sensations through the floor the way I could feel them through my skin?

Sometimes I would be gripped by a panic that seemingly had no impetus. The sensation began in my chest and pulsed continuously down my torso and legs, out my arms and fingertips. When this happened, there was no position I could assume that would alleviate the acute pain. I squirmed on the floor, contorting into all kinds of positions, searching for the magic one, crying fitfully.

"I feel trapped in my skin," I shrieked to my mother during one of these episodes. "How do I get out? Help me get out!"

"I don't know how to help you," she said, trembling, "Call the psychiatrist."

I called my unfeeling psychiatrist and told him, "I feel like I can't breathe. I have pain in my chest that is spreading through my whole body." Meanwhile, my voice felt separate from me as I said all of this, and I was wondering how I was able to say these things and they were able to mean something. I really didn't know how much longer I could keep living like this.

"It sounds like you might need to go to a psychiatric hospital," he said matter-of-factly. "You can check yourself in twenty-four hours a day."

"Okay…" I stammered and hung up.

Still panicked, I told my mom he had suggested the hospital. She asked me if I wanted to go. I didn't want to go; I wanted to be with her. But I didn't know what to do.

"Take some deep breaths," she said, "Let's go to Rite Aid and see if they have any kind of herbal calming pill," she suggested.

Herbal calming pill?! That did *not* sound effective, but I wanted her to take care of me, to tell me what to do to feel better. So we went to the drugstore and purchased a bottle of homeopathic Hyland's Calms Forte.

"How about a warm washcloth for your head?" she said when we got home. "That always helped you calm down as a child."

"Okay." I lay down in her bed while she fetched a warm washcloth for me. I tried to focus on breathing deeply in and out. When my mother stopped fighting me to snap out of it and nurtured me with parental love, I calmed down, bit by bit. I was so relieved not to be alone anymore in the cold, dark, crowded city.

As months passed, working at Round Table gradually became something steady I could depend on. Being engaged in repetitive mindless tasks like making pizza relaxed my brain and gave me something simple on which to focus, with a clear attainable goal. I didn't get jumbled up reading the toppings and their weights off the order ticket. I started to relax a little more around my coworkers and was less nervous talking to customers. At home, I took up similarly mindless therapeutic activities like paint-by-number, jigsaw puzzle making, and sewing, which I worked on obsessively.

As I acclimated to my life's newfound simplicity, my anxiety gradually decreased. But it was slow going; it took almost a year before any semblance of self really returned. Over time, as my stress levels reduced and I felt cared for, my obsession with language began to dissipate. First there was a minute, then an hour, then a few hours, then whole days when I didn't think about it. But I was still dissatisfied and restless, craving a catharsis that psychotherapy and prescription medication could not provide.

On Passover that year, my grandmother came to stay with us. One morning we were sitting across the dining room table and she was helping me brainstorm possible life options, seeing as we both agreed Round Table was not my career destiny. The idea of massage therapy came up. My experience with physical theater training at NYU had sparked this initial interest. We would partner up, one of us lying on the ground, the other pressing on that person's back, pulling and stretching limbs, rolling on the person. The idea was to get the actor to relax and become present in his body. Receiving this work always put me in a delightful trance. I didn't deliberate over the idea of studying massage: I knew intuitively that it was a path I wanted to pursue. I enrolled that fall.

Healer, Heal Thyself

Dear Massage,

Thank you for teaching me how to receive. To release my arms and legs to gravity and let someone else pick them up and move them without my resisting. For warming me with your hands, re-circulating my blood, bringing the color back into my face. For elongating my tissues, pouring fresh oxygen to every cell. For teaching me to breathe into the tight sore spots. To give over, to let go. Touch is relief. When someone places a palm on my sternum and rubs in a gentle circular motion, I almost always cry.

Alone in the massage room, I disrobed completely and placed my clothes on the chair in the corner. The lights were dim and the music was soothing, cradling me in its low hums, lilting lutes, and soft piano. I tiptoed across the cold bamboo floor to the massage table, climbed up, and slipped my shivering naked body stomach down between the sheets. Soothed by sheepskin padding and a warm heating pad, I inhaled my first breath of calm and exhaled a deep sigh of relief.

The massage therapist knocked lightly and entered the room. I closed my eyes as her hands rested gently on my back over the sheet. All she had done so far was lay her hands on my back and I was already relieved, awed by the power of touch, of simple human contact. She was going to take care of me.

"Take a deep breath," she said, and I breathed into her hands.

With one hand on my sacrum and one on my mid-thoracic spine, she began to rock me gently, creating a wave of full-body oscillations. She then pulled the sheet down to my waist, exposing my back. Her warm, oiled palms pressed and glided firmly along my skin. Then she began to slowly and carefully knead my muscles. The music hummed and chimed. My consciousness softened. My body was limp, fully receptive to this woman's manipulations. Her hands moved up and down my back. Kneaded my shoulders. Stretched my limbs. Wrung my hamstrings. My thoughts were dissolving, mind focusing entirely on the physical contact, tracing the pathway of her hands along my body. My heart rate slowed. Tension melted. Eyes rested against my lids, soft black cushions. Mind drifted off. Each muscle group was worked deeply, fully, from head to toe. I was profoundly grateful for these sensations, amazed at how good I could feel in my body. I wanted to be the one to facilitate for others this much-needed reprieve.

At age twenty-three, I enrolled in the School of Healing Arts for massage, a five-hundred-hour program where I was immersed in the world of holistic therapies. I learned about what it means to heal the whole person, mind, body, and spirit, as opposed to standard Western medicine, which compartmentalizes the body and the mind, often treating just diseases and not whole people.

Compassionate teachers introduced me to touch as medicine. I learned to quiet my mind by sitting still with my eyes open and listening for the farthest sound. I learned to give selflessly, lengthening muscles and creating space between tissues. An ounce of prevention is worth an infinite amount of cure. Deep breaths massage us from the inside.

After completing my first two hundred hours of the program, I was eligible for my work permit. I obtained it immediately and started working at a spa called SK Sanctuary, named for its owner, Stephen Krant. The name "sanctuary" couldn't have been more apt; the place was beautiful with its roses, chandeliers, salmon-colored walls, and silver-framed Victorian paintings.

My favorite thing about SK Sanctuary was its monthly breast cancer night. The spa closed to the public, open only for breast cancer patients and survivors. Participants received two free half-hour services, and dynamic speakers on topics like therapeutic dance, singing, yoga for cancer patients, support groups, food, and new cancer study developments. There were occasional music or dance performances. These women's bodies had been diseased, poked, prodded, radiated, chemotherapied, surgeried; they were in deep need of a healing touch.

One particular night, the topic was the therapeutic value of music making. The speakers passed out percussive instruments to all the staff and spa-robed attendees. There were bongos, xylophones, maracas, drums of varying shapes and sizes. The women in charge led us in beating the instruments and raising our voices in unison. I joined the breast cancer survivors in singing, screaming, pounding. We hollered and laughed.

When it was over, I found my client by way of her name tag.

"Hi, I'm Amanda." I smiled and shook her hand. She appeared to be in her mid-thirties, short dirty blonde hair scraggily growing back after chemo. Her handshake was both solid and soft.

"Lucy," she said.

I walked her back to the dimly lit massage room, replete with carpeted floor and three-bulb chandelier. I had lit one tea candle and placed it in a purple glass, which sat comfortably on the marble counter next to the sink. Soft Sanskrit chants and the sound of bells echoed off the walls.

"How are you doing tonight, Lucy?"

"Oh, great," she said. "It's so wonderful that you do this."

"I'm glad you were able to make it! When was the last time you had a massage?"

She thought for a second. "Probably about a year ago."

"Wow, well it's time, then. Are there any particular places causing you discomfort today?"

"Ughh, my whole *body* aches! I had a double mastectomy just a month ago, so I think I will need a pillow under my chest in order to lie flat. My neck and shoulders are especially tight. Really anything you could do would be welcome." She said all this, not as a complaint, but in the way that we report mundane grievances to friends, like, "Oh, the line at the bank was so long," or "Can you believe it, Ben and Jerry's was out of my favorite ice cream."

She smiled at me. I smiled back.

"All right, well, I am going to have you start face down underneath the sheet to focus on your back and shoulders. Then I'll flip you over and we'll do some neck work, then scalp and face. Sound good?"

"Oh, yes, please, anything."

"Great. So place your robe on that hook. I'll be right back."

When I returned she said, "The table is so warm, I feel better already." Standing at Lucy's side, I placed my hands gently on her back over the sheet, one at the bottom of the lumbar spine, one at the top of the thoracic. While my palms rested there and warmed these spots, I asked her to take two deep, full breaths, to send the breath to every cell of her body, helping her to become fully present in the room. Her back rose and fell under my hands. I breathed with her.

After three deep breaths, I peeled off my hands and walked to stand behind the top of her head. I pressed her shoulders gently away from her neck, then, with the heel of my hand, began a series of focused compressions into the muscles from the shoulders down to the sacrum on either side of the spine. I pressed the sacrum gently away, creating length through her vertebrae.

I pulled the sheet down to her waist and tucked it under her hipbones, exposing her back. Coated my hands in the heated massage oil. Rubbed my palms together fast to create heat. Ran my hands from her shoulders to her waist, up the sides of her body, back up her neck. I pulled with my fingertips at the occipital ridge, the crook where the neck meets the skull, creating length. Then I clasped my hands into fists around her hair and pulled lightly at the scalp. I repeated these warm up-strokes four times, prepping the skin and muscles for deeper work.

Firmer pressure. Forearm strokes. Leaning into her muscles.

"Is this pressure okay?" I asked.

"Yes, thank you."

Hooking the upper trapezius with my forearms and sustaining the pressure all down the back, slow and deep, I felt the muscles begin to quiver and release. She breathed. I breathed.

The muscles along her spine (erector spinae) were taut at first. I placed my left thumb over my right and sank into the muscle at the top of the back, allowing the muscle to accept me. Not forcing my way. Then it began to loosen, pulling me along its river down to the bottom of her back.

I tucked a rolled-up towel under the front of her shoulder so the scapula was elevated. Ironing the underside with my forearm, I reached my thumbs beneath the blade and moved slowly up and down, feeling the muscles snap, shift, pop beneath. Her inhalations and exhalations had become much more full as she fell deeper into relaxation.

She breathed in the deepest breath yet and exhaled a long, slow sigh through her mouth. My thumbs sank deeper.

"God, this feels amazing," she said. "I really haven't felt this good in so long. Thank you so much."

Her voice sounded so raw, so full of feeling, it surprised me. Tears pooled in the corners of my eyes. I breathed in and exhaled a long, slow sigh of my own. I shut my eyes as my thumbs continued to bump along her tight muscles.

"Thank *you*," I said.

Reprieve.

Inside a Box Inside a Hole

I was naked under a sheet while Jeff rubbed oil all over my body. We hadn't even kissed yet. After two dates, he invited me to his house to give me a massage. I had never practiced tantra but thought it must feel something like this. After the massage I got dressed, went into the other room, and calmly thanked him, determined not to tear his clothes off. We went out into his garden, sat on the edge of his fishpond, and had our first kiss in the moonlight.

I met Jeff at massage school. He was twenty-nine, six feet tall, and skinny with blue eyes and short sandy-blond hair. Our first few months together were pure bliss. He made the chemicals in my body stir themselves, hormones exploding. I wanted to swallow him; I couldn't get enough. He had such soft skin. Chest to chest. Hips to hips. Bodies aligned. Slow entry. Synchronized rhythms. Overwhelming presence. Breathing in and out. Skyline all lit up against the night outside his window.

Inside the Mind of a Dead Dad:
It's dark in here. I haven't seen the sky in three days. And although I looked in the mirror those same three days ago, I can't remember what my face looks like. It's probably because the man staring back at me was not me. Or maybe it's that I was not him. I can't remember. It doesn't matter.

Being with Jeff liberated me from years of sexual apprehension, which began with my first sexual encounter at age twelve. It was over the weekend of a friend's Bar Mitzvah while my girlfriend Celia and I were staying in Jake's family's guest room in Los Angeles. Jake was the nice Jewish boy with whom we went to summer camp. Daniel was his "bad" friend from school, who smoked weed, drank beer, and tongue-kissed girls. This was the first time I met him. I thought he was cute, with his short curly brown hair, brown eyes, and thin frame. We hit it off immediately and flirted outside during most of the Saturday morning service. As the four of us were walking back to Jake's house afterward, Daniel whispered in my ear, "Can I finger-bang you?" I wasn't entirely sure what finger banging was but fancied myself a rebel, and he was cute, so I said, "Sure."

"My older brothers do this all the time," he said. We stopped in the middle of the sidewalk with Celia and Jake standing beside us. I nervously caught sight of Daniel's grubby index finger before he reached his hand under my blue cotton dress, slid my underwear to the side, and slipped it into my tight twelve-year-old vagina. We walked for a few steps with his finger inserted into me. So this was what finger banging was all about. At first I felt sexy, then embarrassed, then a bit of both. After a few steps, he removed his finger. Jake looked at Celia and said, "I want to try."

When we got back to the house, we all went into Jake's room, where I made out with Daniel on the floor and Celia made out with Jake on the bed, while each finger-banged us. Then we switched: me with Jake and Celia with Daniel. I was both exhilarated and repulsed by the whole experience. When we went to the Bar Mitzvah party later that night, bouncing around to Alanis Morissette's "You Oughta Know," I both prided and berated myself for being a secret slut. Thus commenced my confused relationship with sexuality, a simultaneously intoxicating and shameful pursuit.

As I progressed through my teenage and college years, I came to enjoy all the parts leading up to sex, but when it came to thoughts of actual intercourse, I'd become horrified. Potent fears of pregnancy, AIDS, genital warts, HPV, chlamydia, gonorrhea, syphilis, swollen breasts, bloody nipples, fractured lymph nodes, gastrointestinal failure: high school sex education summoned all these terrors. It was reminiscent of the time I took health in second grade and learned about skin cancer; I was acutely afraid to go into the sun, convinced if I did, I would die. I used to write in my diary, "Dear God, please make it cloudy today, just for me," and hid under awnings at pool parties. I was aware that other people could be in the sun, no problem. But I couldn't risk it. (At eight years old, my parents took me to my first therapist.) Similarly, I was aware that other people on the planet had sex all the time and were still healthy, but I was convinced I would be the one to contract a horrifying affliction.

It's raining. I can hear and feel the drops pattering against this pine box. Outside, a crowd is gathering. I wish I could speak to them, say something, anything. But it's as if my jaw has been wired shut. I am done saying things. The combination of the rain and the wood has made it smell like mildew down here. It is not a pleasant smell. I can't feel my fingers. If I could, I would bring them to my nose to block out the odor.

I lost my virginity drunk on the bathroom floor of a motel at the age of seventeen after a high school dance. I'd been infatuated with Josh all year, and while he had flirted with me heavily, he never asked me out and was dating a small blonde sophomore. But high school was almost over, and all this sexual tension had been mounting; now we were drunkenly slobbering all over each other, sloppily ripping off our clothes. A horde of our drunk friends were in the room right outside the door. We didn't use a condom. "Should we stop?" he asked. "No," I grunted, possessed by carnal cravings. When I woke up the next morning realizing what had happened, I was shocked at my behavior. I could feel the genital warts implanting, started mentally preparing for my first abortion, hyperventilating at the thought of testing HIV positive. How could I have been so careless?

He didn't say a word to me over breakfast with our group of friends at Denny's. He wouldn't even look at me.

After breakfast, coated in nervous sweats, I drove to my doctor's office to get my first morning after pill. Were they going to ask me weird questions? Call my mother? My heart was thumping. The woman at the front desk was sorting papers. Could she tell just by looking that a penis had squirted a terminal illness into me and I might soon be dead?

"Can I help you?" she asked.

"Um…"

"Yes…"

"I need a morning after pill," I mumbled. At least I would die without the shame of teenage pregnancy.

"Okay," she said, "I'll need to see your insurance card, and you'll have to fill out this form."

"You're not going to tell my mom, are you?"

"No," she said.

"Thank you."

Having been initiated into the sex and morning after pill club, I was different now—I was a woman. So far, being a woman was an uncomfortable, alienating experience.

I was predominately celibate during college, slept with just two people in four years, and I was afraid both times. I'd never had a real boyfriend.

Above I hear the soles of shoes crunching dead leaves. There are many people up there. Their chatter echoes in my ears. But it is a controlled sort of chatter, not like the kind at amusement parks or malls. It reminds me of zombies. I am uncomfortable. I want to roll over onto my side, but this box is too constricting. I resolve to make do on my back. What's my alternative?

Then along came Jeff. During our first months together, there were candles, mix CDs, cards, dinners, sunsets, flowers, naked nights in the hot tub, shooting stars. It was syrupy and disgusting, and, having never experienced anything like it, I devoured it. Days became about how long it would be before we saw each other again. Seeing him ignited electric surges all through my body. We sent text messages like "I miss you" after parting two hours before. Texts where he called me "Sweet precious angel" and with quotes like "Out beyond ideas of wrongdoing and rightdoing, there is a field. I will meet you there."—Rumi. Then in person, my name became "Babe." Having never gone by "Babe" before, I started to see myself as a rich new brand of feminine; I enjoyed being somebody's "Babe." So in love I thought my heart would explode, I became a love junkie; the more I got, the more I wanted. For so long, there had been this empty pit inside me, a persistent gnawing absence. Now here was Jeff, filling me up. Obsessed, I fell hard, face first, and lost myself entirely.

Jeff had an insatiable interest in Eastern philosophy and religion. His bookshelves teemed with books on Hinduism, Buddhism, Taoism, enlightenment, self-realization: *The Bhagavad-Gita*, *Tao Te-Ching*, books by Paramahansa Yogananda, J. Krishnamurti, Osho. He meditated regularly. His house was a perfect manifestation of feng shui, all Eastern in design, rich in color and texture. There were potted plants, pillows of all shapes and sizes to varying degrees of softness, incense, candles, Buddha statues, rugs, the most luxuriously soft blankets my hands had ever touched, Om signs, paintings of landscapes—purple, blue, green, gold. The house was often flooded by Eastern melodies: Buddhist and Hindu chants, meditative dirges. He also had a stunning garden that he regularly worked in, bundles of long vines strung through the fence and gate, budding with fresh pink flowers. Potted plants of the deepest green. Huge trees. Tibetan prayer flags hung taut above, suspended between his upstairs terrace railing and a tree trunk on the other side of the garden. I found the whole thing quite romantic, plunged into his beautiful, mystical world.

He used to read to me from Osho's *Book of Secrets* before bed. (Osho is an "enlightened" twentieth-century Indian philosopher who developed several of his own unique meditation techniques.) He had a talent for reading meditations; the words, nourished by his warm voice, sailed slowly through his lips with delicate precision. The house was quiet and still. All lights were out except for the reading lamp on his side of the bed. I slid comfortably between his fresh clean purple sheets, under his delicious taupe down comforter. As he began to read, I closed my eyes and listened. *"When you take your breath in, you never feel the breath. You have never felt the breath."* His voice was lilting, soothing as usual. I took slow deep breaths and focused on the words. *"You will immediately deny this. You will say, 'This is not right. We may not be conscious continuously, but we feel the breath.' No, you do not feel the breath, you feel the passage. Look at the sea. Waves are there; you see the waves. But those waves are created by air, wind…"* Gradually I began to drift from consciousness… His voice started mingling with my half dreams… The bed was becoming soft, velvety black quicksand… My body was sinking, sinking… His voice… And then, he stopped. He moved closer to me. My eyes still closed, I could hear him breathing. Then, softly, "I love you, Amanda," he said. "I know you already know, but I wanted to say so now." My heart was warm and melting, spreading through my chest, into my back, down to my fingers and toes. I opened my eyes slowly and looked up into his. "I love you, too," I said.

Squish. Squish. Shoes against dirt turned to mud from the rain. I think about my children. I have three: two daughters and a son. My daughters are fourteen and seventeen. My son is ten. I think about my wife. She is tending to the guests. She wants to make sure everyone feels comfortable, as comfortable as they can feel, given the situation.

Submerged in Jeff's sticky seductive sap, I didn't realize I was allowing myself to become just another ornament in his Eastern landscape, a throw pillow, a decorative emblem. I don't think he ever really knew me or wanted to know me. But I think we were both guilty, each projecting an idealized partner onto the other person. I was so in love with the idea of being in love. This was all new territory, this relationship land. But after a few months, his sweet texts stopped coming, along with the flowers, the kisses, and ultimately the sex. As Jeff withdrew, I challenged him, trying to force him into being close to me again.

"Why don't you want to have sex with me?"

"It's not about you. I just don't feel particularly sexual right now."

I didn't buy it. I didn't know why he couldn't just be honest with me. It hurt so much that I had finally allowed myself to become sexually vulnerable, finally felt taken care of that way, and was now being rejected. I wanted him to be how he was at the beginning, but he wouldn't concede.

All his Eastern fetishism, which had initially seemed romantic, began to grate on my nerves. I started to see it as cheesy, to realize he was the only child of well-to-do real estate agent parents who owned the house he lived in, and that he used all this supposed mysticism as a substitute for pursuing any real life goals. He smoked pot and experimented with hallucinogenic drugs to help him have "visions." I noticed these things, was irked by them, and then lied to myself, because wasn't it nice to be with someone? I continued to think this way even as he became condescending, implying that my wisdom could never match his.

"You should work on your mind," he'd say. "Re-examine the things you think and why you think them."

"You should, too," I retorted.

"I have been," he said snidely, "for the last eight years."

Still, I suppressed my irritation and continued to love him, projecting the delicious gooiness of those first few months onto him, becoming progressively more passive, drifting further away from myself into a frame on his wall.

I hear my son whining, "I'm hungry."

"You'll have to wait," replies my wife in careful even tones.

"I'm so sorry," someone says to her. It's a voice that I don't recognize.

"Thank you." My wife again.
Then all their words stream into the winding current of empty chatter.

There were several mornings I cried at the breakfast table, after Jeff and I had gone to sleep without any physical affection and I'd woken up thinking sex might happen then, but he'd hopped out of bed and into the shower.

"I miss you," I'd say. "Where are you? Why don't you want to be with me?"

He wouldn't touch me or hug me while I sat there, crying. His physical form felt drained of spirit, blue eyes staring vacantly at me like I was an inanimate object. This was who he really was, and that sweet, generous person I'd fallen for was a façade. I wanted to turn the proverbs he spouted into ropes with which to wring his neck. I should have been the one to end it, but he kept saying "I love you," and I was addicted to hearing it. He said other things, too, like, "Let go of your expectations about this relationship. Remain unattached."

I thought these were pretty crappy lines to feed a girlfriend and didn't think even Buddha would approve. But unfortunately for me, I *had* become attached. So-called love had transitioned into desperate clinging and obsession. Finally, Jeff rolled over in bed on a morning that followed another sexless night and said, "I can't give you what you deserve. I need to let you go now." The morning light leaked in from between his maroon curtains. The room was cold.

I soaked his pillows with snot and tears, body convulsing. It felt like my innards were collapsing and being slowly ripped from me as he hugged me and kept saying, "I love you. I'm sorry."

"You mean so much to my life, I've learned so much because of you," I said, hugging him back while wanting to rip his face off. It was quite disorienting to experience such opposing extremes at once.

I drove to the beach, parked my car, and ran down to the sand. I pulled off my socks and shoes, rolled up my pants, and stomped through the water. Sun beating down. I dipped my hands in the ocean and anointed my face and arms, crying with passionate force. Body quaking. The water was freezing, like needles against my skin. I cupped the water in my palms and dumped it on my head, running my fingers through my hair. Streams poured down the sides of my face. I dunked my arms in up to my shoulders, rocking back and forth, crying with my whole body.

"Are you okay? Do you need any food or money?" a stranger asked me. "No," I grunted. He went on his way. My chest and abdomen felt like they had been struck by boulders.

Night after night, I was jerked from sleep by panic attacks. I flopped around the mattress, trying to breathe, but my mind repeated the same thoughts: How could this person mysteriously appear, becomes the focal point of my whole existence, then retreat and disappear, morphing into ghost form, leaving me and my subconscious alone to combat the memories? I was sucked into a violent cycle of reinterpreting his language and behavior, futile attempts to figure out what went on inside his head, what his true feelings and motivations were. I could speculate forever, a totally useless mental exercise, like wondering what the moon would look like from Jupiter.

My mind was reeling; I couldn't stop thinking about him and feared I would have to resign my life to this newfound handicap. I writhed in sleepless and foodless anguish for weeks, attacked by memories of first encounter, first date, first kiss, first sex, first I-love-you. If I were lucky enough to get to sleep, I would wake with squeezing and gripping sensations. So this was what a broken heart felt like.

I would lie in bed in the dark, shut my eyes, and feel his phantom body resting on mine. I'd squirm and shift, unable to will it off me, copulating with his ghost all through the night.

I realized later that this all had little to do with Jeff as a person. It was all about what he represented and what he stirred up in me, a barrel full of major firsts: first real relationship, first taste of sexual freedom. Trust. Vulnerability. Nakedness. All these previously caged feelings had been awakened and were now spinning at the surface.

One night as I was lying in bed amongst the then-familiar knots, I felt a sudden sharp pain in my side. I missed my father. The pain traveled to my other side. My father had been dead for seven years. What did breaking up with a boyfriend have to do with him? Something about the grief I was experiencing was tapping into a well of preexisting grief. I wanted to eject all this feeling; it was too big. I was consumed by thoughts of my father. I wanted to run to him, hug him, talk to him. I couldn't. The two losses were colliding, one face superimposed on the other. All this grief had been dammed up inside feelings associated with love and sexuality. As those walls were breached and then torn down, everything began to flow, to flood.

I run my tongue, rough as sandpaper, across the roof of my mouth. I try to open my mouth. I can't. I swallow. But there is no fluid in my system, which means no saliva. I think I am swallowing, but really it's just my throat contracting. And then I lose all feeling in my throat. I forget what a throat even is.

Mourning happens in waves forever. It's never done. Survivors are like amputees; the deceased become phantom limbs. Loss pools with loss. Grief tumors implant in the intestines, beneath the sternum and inside the heart, and flare up when tapped. Sublingual. Irrational. Unscientific. Contemplating death is like contemplating the magnitude of the universe; the brain rejects it.

When things are open, the air comes through. Sometimes the air is cold and burns. The way Jeff pressed himself onto me, into me, filled me up. The way he pulled out and withdrew, it was reminiscent of my father dying.

The chatter stops.
The voices trump together in unison:

We aver, despite our woe, that life is good and life's tasks must be performed. Help us, O Lord, to rise above our sorrow and face the trials of life with courage in our hearts. Give us insight in this hour of grief, that from the depth of suffering may come a deepened sympathy for all who are bereaved, that we may feel the heartbreak of our fellowmen and find our strength in helping them...'

After the breakup, I was arrested by pained lust. At work, buzzing. Car—buzzing. Street—buzzing. Visions of ears. Lips, teeth, tip of the tongue—pink and wet in the mouth, rolling along the edges of the gums. Muscles. Bones. Human anatomy! My body wrapped up inside someone else's. In, on top of, inside, under, rolling rolling, melting melting, sugar sweet. Full body pulse, belting arias and hitting the highest notes—Italian sky. Urban sky. Country sky. Skyline. Kiss me, kiss me, KISS ME! Sideways—hot hot. First the breath, then the lips, then the tongue. In and through. Flood. Standing on the bridge, entranced by the view. Standing on the roof. SO MUCH SKY! SO MANY STARS!   One two three JUMP!!! (The perfect time to grow wings.) Night. Sky. Air. Moon. Giant blast of Mercury out my window. Seemingly unrelated. "All things are one," I told him, would tell him, if he would listen. Sit. Stand. Lie. Kiss. Licking. Moving. Music. Sing. A torrent. A whishhhh. A what? Oh oh please yes please thank you. Delicious. Rich. Full. Sweet. Strawberry dripping chocolate into my mouth. mouth. mouth. mouth. *Jeff always dressed his messages in stars*

Unfortunately, my lust was accompanied by the vengeful return of my sexual apprehensions, and the combination was unnerving. I went home with a guy I met at a bar; this was a first. I'd gone alone, deliberately sought it out. We stumbled outside, and he lit a cigarette. He had sleeves of tattoos down both his arms. His brown eyes glowed under the bar's door light.

By 3 a.m., I had become acquainted with his naked body: His arms and legs were covered in tattoos, and both his nipples were pierced. My shirt was off, and he was kissing my skin. Trailing torso to hips, delicately kissing each hipbone. Everyone has his own sweet things that he does. Soon we were both naked, and then we were having sex, and I wanted it until I didn't. I was hovering above myself, watching myself screw this stranger, and after a few minutes I began to panic, I had to stop. I couldn't keep going, despite my fear of guilt and embarrassment. Ultimately, it didn't matter what he thought. He didn't know me; he didn't care about me. I really wanted him off me.

"Can we stop?"

"What, why? Are you serious?"

"Yeah, it's not you, I just need to stop. I'm sorry."

I try to picture the inside of my brain infested with roaches and maggots. It is near impossible to conjure such an image. But as I try, I actually start to feel things crawling around in there. Slimy things, dragging their bodies along the walls of my skull, leaving a trail of excrement behind them. I feel the excrement gushing out my ears; the pine box teems to overflowing with this flux of maggot feces. I feel myself start to gag, but then I stop because I have lost my throat. I gag in spite of myself.

After two months of not speaking to Jeff, one of my empowerment strategies was to reclaim the stage. I performed a solo act at San Diego's Bluefoot Bar in their monthly performance series, *4x4*. Each person had ten minutes to perform anything: music, song, dance, spoken word, performance art. That month was Ladies' Night. I performed a Gilda Radner sketch: "The Judy Miller Show." A hyper young brownie scout, I shrieked through a show in my bedroom for no one in particular after my parents banished me from their bridge game downstairs. Then, transitioning into Judy's grown-up self, I put on a poufy white lace dress and passionately sang a folk song to a Ken doll, her husband to be. It had been years since I had performed solo like this, and it felt great.

After the show, I was being congratulated and riding out my adrenaline when Jeff appeared out of nowhere. I knew he was a friend of Jill, a local dancer affiliated with the performance series, and I knew she would be there. I had a slight hunch that he might show up, and I had played it out in my head a few times, but he was always so surrealistic in these dreamscapes, some kind of distorted half-human version of himself that never fully translated into real life. But there he was, just casually strolling up next to me, as if he'd been resurrected. He had cut his hair, he looked even thinner than I remembered, his arms two long sticks poking out of the sleeves of his white V-neck T-shirt. As always, he was wearing his Buddha beads under his shirt, the top part peering out around the back of his neck.

"Hi, how have you been?" His laughably non-casual attempt at casual conversation. Every muscle in my body felt wooden.

"Oh, I'm fine, how have you been?"

Remember how we used to fuck and say "I love you"? Crazy, right? Gosh, how have you been?

"Fine."

You know what else is crazy, all the times your dick's been in my mouth! Nice weather, huh?

"Good, what's new?"

Douchenut. Douchebag. Douchesalad. Douchehole. Douchedick. Shit-douche. Dickteeth. Pubic hair face. Pubic hair neck. Assholetoolbelt.

"Well, Chris and his band have been down from L.A. staying with me for the last few days. They were playing music until 3 a.m. this morning; it was great. Then we all woke up early and went to a yoga class…" *Blah blah blah.*

Fuck you, I hate you, I love you, I hate you, I love you, fuck you, let's fuck… I hate you. I love you. Fuck you. Fuck me.

We stood there awkwardly for a moment or so.

"Well, I'm going to go find my friend," Jeff said and brushed past me.

The friend I was with promptly ushered me out of there and dragged me in my hysteria to another bar. As I was leaving Blue-foot, Jeff saw me, and we engaged in a ten-second nonsensical waving ritual. After chugging three vodka tonics and wailing to my friend for over half an hour, it was after midnight and she had to work early in the morning, so she drove me back to my car.

I should have just gotten in and drove home, but I decided I would go back over to Bluefoot to bum a cigarette. I don't make a habit of smoking, in light of my father's death. But it was my excuse to try to run into him again. I think there is something inherently masochistic in human nature that makes us torture ourselves in this way. Like the way I keep my relationship in a bag in the garage, all Jeff's mix CDs, cards, and gifts that I periodically go back and look through, which is like drinking petroleum every time. I should have just gotten in my car and gone home. But I couldn't resist.

As I was rushing past the bar entrance, Jeff was stepping out—really, just like that.

"Oh, hi," I stammered.

"Hi…what are you still doing here?"

"Oh, I went to another bar and just came back to bum a ciga-rette."

And then I stopped and really looked at him; there was a morbid fascination with what was taking place. I felt all the pain well up, converge, and explode; I wanted to hug him forever and cut off his nut sack all at once.

He hugged me, and I just melted. I hadn't seen or touched him for two months, and the familiarity of that body…I fell fully into the moment, not thinking about its looming repercussions.

Just let me stay here forever.

And then he let go.

The sky fades from blue-gray to gray to black. Not a single star tonight. The tears mingle with the rain and water the lawn. The rain stops. A shooting star passes overhead. A grunt is heard in the crowd. It is an old man throwing out his back. His wife escorts him to the car. Everyone decides it is time to go home.

"I just want you to know I haven't been dating other people since we broke up," he said.

"Uh-huh."

"It was never about that, wanting to date other people. I just wasn't in a good place to be in a relationship anymore; I needed to go inward."

"Uh-huh."

We hugged again.

"I love you," he had the nerve to say.

"I love *you*," I said, cowardly.

"Well, I have to go. My friends are waiting for me."

I glanced around the corner at three gorgeous girls, two of them blonde, one whom he'd introduced earlier as his new room-mate back at our initial awful run-in.

"Okay." I was in shock; all my body systems had shut down.

"Don't get lost in here," he pointed to his head. So patronizing. So much "wisdom." He was really on "the path." As if he had the right to tell me how to feel.

I didn't say anything. I just watched him link arms with the girls, round the corner, and disappear.

I finally bummed that cigarette, sat on the ground outside the bar, and screamed to the sky, literally. I screamed out loud on the ground outside the bar. It didn't seem to bother any of the drunks on the terrace. How could he just reappear like that and abandon me again?

But before anyone can leave, each person takes a turn dumping a shovelful of dirt over the coffin, as is the custom in Judaism. Wet and shivering, the people wait in line for their turn. My family stands to the side of the grave, opposite the crowd, and graciously receives each individual's condolences. Fifty-some shovels' worth of dirt later, everyone but my family has left. It is dark and cold, even for November, especially for San Diego.

As I picked myself up from the ground and scampered to my car, I began calling him incessantly. Once. No answer. Twice. Still no answer. Desperation had trumped integrity. I was going to keep calling until he had the balls to pick it up. Finally on the fourth call he answered.

"Hello, I'm at dinner."

"Yeah, well, I just really want to talk to you. I wasn't expecting to see you, and it really hurt to see you there like that tonight."

"I'm sorry. Look, I'm at dinner with people, and I can't talk right now."

I heard one of the girls in the background giddily say, "Jeff, get off the phone, you're being rude. Heehee."

"But I want to talk to you," I whined, drained of sanity. I couldn't let this go.

I can hear my wife breathing. I can smell her deodorant. I catch a strong whiff before my olfactory passages cease function altogether. My nose has gone out dancing somewhere with my throat. But I don't have a throat.

Has this pine box already begun to decay? How long have I been in here? I've grown weary. Perhaps I ought to rest my eyelids. I don't have eyelids. I don't have eyes. I see nothing. So long to the pounding in my skull, the incessant thumping.

"Mom, let's go." My son again.

"Yeah, come on, Mom." My middle daughter.

"It's about time." My oldest daughter.

The hovering-above version of myself was shaking her head at me, saying, "Darling, please stop." But I couldn't stop. I didn't really know what I wanted to talk about with him, except that I wanted to keep talking to him. I craved closure. But that really was impossible in this situation.

"If you want, we can set up a phone conversation in the morning, but don't call before 11:00," he said.

We can set up a phone conversation! What a charitable fellow. Well, after this ridiculous offer, he hung up on me. Then he text-messaged me, "Thank you. Sincerely. I am sorry if you are hurt."

What a high and mighty prince of Tibet. I couldn't let it go, just brush my hands together, pack up and go home, saying, *Oh, okay, so that's that. On with my life.* No, I kept calling. He didn't pick up. Finally after the third call I left a message.

"Look, I just think what you did tonight was really rude and selfish. Fuck this… Damnit, I wish I wasn't leaving this message."

He called me back around 6 p.m. the next night for what would be our last conversation. For months, the concluding sentence resounded in my brain: "Well, maybe I'll talk to you again someday." Click. He was gone.

My wife blows me a kiss. The smack of her lips echoes as it hits the air. My pine box reverberates beneath a mound of dirt. This kiss is the last thing I hear before my ears collapse in on themselves. Nothing more to see, hear, smell.

I was clawing viciously for my dad, for a hug from him, a kiss on the cheek, to hear his voice. It felt like there was a hand inside my stomach, squeezing and wringing out my guts. Jeff, come back. Touch me. Love me. Dad, come back. Hug me. Lay a hand on my back and sit quietly with me. Kiss me on the cheek. Play a record for me. Let's go for a walk. Dad, Dad, come back. Please. Come back. Dad.

"But before we go…" My wife trails off. She hands my ten-year-old son the shovel. He adds a shovel's worth of dirt to the mound. He passes it off to my middle daughter, who does the same. She passes it off to my oldest daughter, who does the same. She passes it off to my wife, who does the same. I struggle to open my mouth, I can't. I want to call to them, to bestow some parting words. I fight to open my jaw, tongue a-flutter, teeth grinding and starting to break into my mouth. I swallow them dry, no more saliva. My family is walking away. Family! Wait! I can't speak. No concluding sentence. No more saying things. No more voice. No more brain. They are gone.

What Now?

I had to run. I shoved my feet into pre-laced running shoes still caked in the dried muddy film of yesterday's park puddles. Thinking the fresh air and motion would clear up all my mental rumblings and intestinal grievances, I hoisted myself up from the wood-paneled floor and unbolted the door. Swooped down the two dusty flights of stairs to street level. Outside. Wind slap. My feet hit the pavement like bricks, pounding. Hips spinning and popping. Lungs heaving, alveolar sacs expanding and contracting. Blood oxygenating, sparking venous return, heart racing to keep up.

I thought maybe if I ran fast enough, I could shed my skin. Somehow the inertia would become so great that my dermal layer would be seized and ripped off by the wind. Then my blood would gush upon the sidewalk in sheets, organs spilling out one by one. Liver—squish. Gallbladder—splash. Uterus—kerplop. Tendons springing loose, muscles flapping behind until they, too, were torn off. My heart would detach, dangling from cords of veins and arteries until their snap: violent ejection, heart bouncing off the road like a tennis ball (soon to be crushed by a nine-wheeler). All my anatomy would spew out in a trail behind me along the sidewalk as I pummeled past the houses on my way to the park. A skeleton sprinting, I would slam into a tree trunk, bones snapping and flying in all directions.

When I got to the park on this gray morning, anatomy fully intact, I made a mad dash for the lake. Red, orange, gold-leafed trees, vision blurred, colors swirling, I ran right up to the muddy edge, crunching dead leaves along the way. I stopped abruptly, folded over my legs, panting. Cyclists and runners streamed along the road through the park. But luckily, no one was stationed anywhere near me. So I jerked my torso back up to standing, took a deep breath, threw my hands in the air and belted out the deepest fullest sound of which my body was capable. Its force shook the space. I flung my arms around, over my head, side to side, jumping in place, hurling kicking motions, flailing as much as my body would allow. Then I took off again, back to my house.

I had taken up running in an effort to diffuse all the explosive anger and hurt. This break up had opened a huge floodgate. It was as if the stitches on all prior wounds had burst open; I felt my emotions gushing. Everything that had ever touched me deeply was converging and exploding: my eating disorder, my father's death, my psychosis, all the creative success I craved so deeply, the aching desire to be loved, my confusion about what direction to take my life. I woke up every morning feeling like I'd been stabbed everywhere and erupted with uncontrollable tears at all hours.

Determined not to collapse into catatonic depression, I devised a healing regimen involving running, psychotherapy, working at the spa, and yoga. I would often be up all night crying and thrashing about in my bed, alternating writing undeliverable letters to Jeff and to my father's ghost, and would leave frantic messages on my therapist's voicemail calling for an emergency session in the morning.

I worked to channel my emotions into helping my massage clients. Long, deep strokes into a woman's back muscles with the heel of my hand transformed sadness and rage into healing. Some sessions were so powerful, I'd become overwhelmed by the way pain transformed into deep love for this naked stranger on my table. I wanted her to be soothed so I could be soothed. If I could fix her, I could fix me. I wept silently through several sessions and bowed my head in profound gratitude as I thanked my client at the end of the hour, my palms resting gently over her eyes. *Thank you for allowing me to focus on you for this hour. May your life be filled with joy and light. I love you.*

I went to yoga class every day. I had practiced yoga on and off since my senior year of high school, when my friend brought me to some classes at a YMCA. I had started to pick it up more routinely since I'd begun studying massage and found it to be enormously helpful in relieving my stress. After the breakup, I became addicted to heated power yoga, where I would sweat vigorously while contorting my body into poses that made my muscles scream and burn. I held poses until the teacher told me I could release, no matter how much pain I was in. The sweating and the pain became masochistic. I pushed myself as far as my body could take it and then a little further, my heart pumping grief through my bloodstream. I cried through most of the classes my first month in attendance.

At the end of the class, in our final resting poses with meditative soundscapes cooing out the speakers, I was usually lying face up on my mat, convulsing with tears. I was embarrassed to be wailing audibly in a room full of strangers, but I couldn't help myself. The teacher was always gracious. She knelt down behind me, lifted up my head, slipped her fingers down to the base of my sweaty neck, and deeply combed the muscles along my cervical vertebrae with her fingertips. Then she pressed my shoulders away, one at a time, and rested her hands against my sternum until my inhales and exhales began to lengthen and my crying reduced to a whimper.

"Thank you for being so open with your emotions," a man said one day as we rolled up our mats after class. He had bright blue eyes and chestnut-brown hair. He was thin and strong. I wanted him to hug me, take me home, make me tea, undress both of us, and wrap his limbs around me under a blanket by a fire. But instead I just wiped my wet cheeks and smiled at him. It was such a small, simple exchange, but I found that brief connection very meaningful; something softened inside me.

I gradually stopped approaching yoga as a means of punishing myself, and came to see it for what it was: a perfect metaphor for how to deal with life. It was about training one's mind to relax under stressful circumstances, accomplished by deepening the breath to help maintain difficult postures and moving with the breath from one posture to another. Yoga literally means union: the union of mind, body, and spirit, encouraging the mind to stop belaboring thoughts about the past and future and embrace the present. I started to find the practice calming and centering; I continued to go every day and stopped crying through the classes. I found myself growing stronger physically, mentally, and spiritually.

As I lay in final resting pose at the end of class, I was flooded by existential questions. Who was I? What was I doing? Where was I going? I examined the facts: twenty-four years old, five foot four and a half inches tall, one hundred and twelve pounds. Hair: a mat of curly Jewish frizz. Eyes: blue. I had two hands, two feet, arms, legs, internal organs, and all the other normal human parts. I was going to keep waking up every day with several conscious hours to fill until it all stopped. I wanted my self to be ignited, irrepressible, for my life to be dynamic and meaningful. At some point, I wanted to be something, marry someone, live somewhere.

I decided it was time for a major upheaval. I needed to get out of my mother's house. Sitting in the garage one afternoon, rummaging through old boxes, I found my papers from the writing program and was gripped by the drive to create; I wanted to complete my degree. After a three-year leave of absence, I made plans to move back to New York. I was not sure exactly what my ultimate path was or what would happen after the master's degree, but I told myself to take one thing at a time. I would continue moving and searching. Only this brain, only this body—we would keep working to get along.

When I moved back to New York, before the semester had even begun, I had started thinking about traveling to India. I'd become so transfixed by yoga that I wanted to study it in its country of origin, learn more about its history and philosophy, and sink deeper into the practice. I realized I was addicted to programs; I couldn't just have hobbies. Any time I became fascinated by a subject, I had to immerse myself in it. I was in the graduate writing program and already researching another program to follow. Searching around the Internet, I found Yoga Vidya Gurukul, an ashram four hours inland from Mumbai.

An ashram is essentially a secluded place in a beautiful natural setting where people come to be part of a community and pursue peace of mind. People pursue this peace by practicing yoga and/or meditation. An ashram is designed for simplicity, to give people what they need and not what they want, to minimize external distractions so people can come to deal with their difficulties head on, moving through them and past them, working toward freeing themselves from their own minds. Yoga Vidya Gurukul was such a place, providing all this, while offering a 250-hour teacher-training course and the opportunity to be immersed in the yogic lifestyle. I wasn't certain I really wanted to be a yoga teacher, but I knew I wanted to bring myself deeper into the practice and that the teaching certificate couldn't hurt. It would cost me seven hundred and fifty dollars for the entire month, including the training, meals, and accommodations, in addition to the plane ticket. I bookmarked the page and let the thought rest in the back of my mind as I resumed my creative writing studies.

I wrote, subjected my writing to workshop criticism, read books, shivered in the winter, took power yoga classes, and toiled with my master's thesis. It was difficult to reacquaint myself with New York City after three years, the place I associated with my meltdown, while simultaneously re-entering the program when everyone was in their second year and had already established groups of friends. I was feeling very insecure socially and didn't get close to anyone. Hence, my thesis became my sole obsession. After struggling with it to the point of wanting to smash my computer with a hammer and swear off writing forever, I started to see it turning into a memoir. I was writing about all the major experiences I'd had in my life that I cared about, that had changed me in some way. I was achieving catharsis through reliving events, writing about them, and letting them go. When I wasn't battling my part-time job in arts administration, I was staring at the computer screen, sinking deeper into memories, trying to find the right words, reworking the same paragraph eight, ten, fifteen times, pounding at the keyboard. Several times, I woke with a start in the middle of the night and jerked my laptop open on the fold-up TV dinner table at the side of my bed. My thesis and I slept together, ate together, talked about everything, laughed and cried together.

Suddenly it was May, and the thesis due date had arrived. I had to stop editing, bind it up, and turn it in. I was having separation anxiety. I didn't want to let it go. I was experiencing similar feelings to when Jeff broke up with me. The thesis had been consuming all my time and attention. I had been able to block out all other thoughts, such as the reality of graduating and the painful question that continued to resurface like an incurable cyst: What now? I turned in my thesis and cried for three days straight.

I got out of bed the fourth morning after the thesis due date, opened my laptop, found the Yoga Vidya Gurukul website, and looked up start dates for the next teacher training course. The next start date that had slots open was September seventeenth. I put the one-hundred-dollar registration fee on my credit card, closed my laptop, and took a shower.

I knew I couldn't go all the way to India without traveling a bit beyond the ashram. Initially, I had planned to travel for ten days before the program on my own. But as I read in my *Lonely Planet* guidebook about the dangers of being a white female traveling alone, I began to reevaluate. I imagined myself robbed, raped, and broken on a train station platform without a cell phone, babbling to strangers who didn't speak my language about how I needed to get to the ashram, as they wriggled off my remaining clothes and left me drooling and spitting up blood. I decided to call up the student travel agency. I spoke to a cheerful British lady who highly recommended a reasonably priced two-week tour with the company GAP Adventures, from Delhi, India, to Kathmandu, Nepal. It would be one week in India and one in Nepal, was for people under age thirty-six, and would finish five days before the teacher-training course began. I would be gone a total of seven weeks.

"You're in luck. There's still one slot left. I'm sure you'll have a lovely time," she said, in a most proper British accent. I hung up the phone, smiled, and sighed. Cheerful British people could sell me anything.

The next morning, I went into work and gave notice that I would be quitting in mid-August. I told my roommate, and the next day she found a friend to sublet my room for September and October. Everything seemed to be falling into place, including my pattern of embarking on temporary thrills without a plan for what follows. "What now?" would be waiting for me at the end of October. I told it to go sniff some glue in the meantime.

This trip would be about building a more solid relationship with myself, letting go of fear, and growing an emotional back-bone. I was fed up with flopping between emotional extremes. I was sick of my mind spinning anxieties out of control and the effects this had on my body, particularly my muscles and my breath. I didn't want to live the rest of my life feeling physical and mental anguish over everything I desired, primarily artistic success and romantic love. I wanted to become better at making decisions, able to move more gracefully through the transitions, and learn to enjoy the journey without self-torture. I believed removing myself from everything familiar would help me gain important perspective on my life and help me really work toward these goals.

My mother was supportive of the trip and helped me to pay for the plane ticket. Bless her, she supports everything I want to do. She wanted me to come home to San Diego before heading out to India so she could see me off. I spent a most enjoyable ten days at home with her, relaxing and giving massages at SK Sanctuary, and after three months of planning and talking about the trip, it was time to go. I was too excited and nervous to sleep the night before departing. I lay awake, trying to process the fact that I would be traveling halfway around the world to a completely foreign place with a different culture and language: all by myself. I figured if I could do this, I could do anything.

Eeendeeaaaah

On a morning in late August, at 8:00 a.m. San Diego time, I sat alone in a plane on a runway. My heart was thumping wildly through my whole body, my armpits were soaked with sweat, and my skull was buzzing. My journey would take twenty-four hours in total: five and a half hours to Newark, a four-and-a-half-hour layover, then fourteen hours from Newark to New Delhi. I was already exhausted from the previous night's insomnia. I opened to the world map in my Continental Airlines magazine and stared at India until the page became blurry. At that point, it was just a shape on a map. There was no way to know what I would see or whom I would meet there. This did feel like a pilgrimage of sorts, plunging myself into the unknown. Wide open. No tangible expectations. Free.

At 7:30 p.m. in the Newark airport, I arrived at the gate to board my fourteen-hour flight to New Delhi. I scanned the waiting area. Nearly everyone was Indian. For the first time in my life, I felt like a cultural outsider. I couldn't hide the color of my skin. I thought about this being the first moment of a feeling that would last all through my travels. I thought about the Indian people sitting in this waiting area, who had immigrated to America, and empathized with the sense of isolation they must have initially felt. What courage.

My heart fluttered. *I can't believe I'm really going.* I plopped down on the ground and swallowed my first malaria pill. Malaria was still an epidemic in India, and it was recommended I take these once a day for prevention. Side effects could include headache and nausea, at least at the beginning. Lo and behold, it took a mere five minutes for nausea to sink in. I wasn't sure how much was psychological, nerves, or the pill itself, but I sure felt woozy, held onto my stomach, and took slow, deep breaths.

A few minutes later, an Indian woman wearing an aquamarine T-shirt and beige cargo pants sauntered up to me. We were dressed almost exactly alike: same clothes, slightly different shades of the same colors. Somehow it felt predestined.

"You're traveling alone?" she asked. I nodded my head yes.

"Brave girl," she said. She had a thin Indian accent, watered down by America.

"Where are you from?" I asked.

"Ohio. You?"

"San Diego, but I live in New York."

She brushed her long frizzy brown ponytail off her shoulder.

"No way, I grew up in Queens! Well, I was born in India, but my parents moved us to New York when I was very young. I'm Shymala."

She sat down and stretched her hand out toward me. I stretched mine out to meet it. Her handshake was firm and excited. I felt my shoulders relax and the nausea subside.

Through the ensuing conversation, I learned that Shymala taught medicine in Ohio and had traveled all over the world, but had never been back to India. Now she was going for a fifteen-day adventure tour with her brother.

"So what are you going to do in India?" she asked me, scooting closer.

"I'm going on a tour for two weeks: one week in India and one in Nepal. Then I'm doing a month-long yoga teacher training on an ashram."

Her brown eyes widened, and her mouth stretched into a giant grin. "Wow, that sounds so cool!"

"Thanks," I said, feeling my nervousness ping-pong back to excitement.

"What's your religion?" she asked.

"I'm Jewish."

She sat up straight and her expression grew serious. "Be careful. Don't talk to any Muslims—people from Pakistan, Iran, and Afghanistan. Lots of them are very dangerous. When I was a little girl, they used to kidnap the prettiest young girls and sell them as slaves. I had eight brothers who protected me."

My excitement was again eclipsed by nervousness. I pictured a crowd of angry Muslim men in turbans holding knives to my neck, head, and face. I tried to imagine the landscape where I might see these people. I had no point of reference. The closest place I had been geographically was Israel. I pictured a Jerusalem where all the women were wearing saris and Bollywood dancing while the men attacked me in a back alley. But nobody could hear the attack to come save me because the Bollywood music was too loud. I felt my breath get caught in my chest as all the color drained from my face.

"I'm not trying to dampen your enthusiasm," she said and reached her warm hand out to rest it on top of mine. "Just be on your guard. You're a young, pretty white girl. Don't go anywhere alone at night. Also, don't let anyone know you are Jewish, and don't reveal too much about yourself."

I nodded and stared at her light brown hand. Her knuckles were stubby and her nails were bitten down short, just like mine.

"Are you a student?" she asked, changing the subject.

"Not anymore. I just finished grad school for creative writing."

"Oh, well, that explains why you would want to go on this trip. These things are good for the creative mind."

I buzzed with excitement once again.

"Well, nice to meet you," she said, removing her hand and hoisting herself up to a squat. "I'm going to get up and walk around a bit before having to sit for fourteen hours."

"Okay, see you soon."

My heart was pounding through my whole body. The colors were swirling around me; everything suddenly seemed brighter and more intense. I looked down at my watch. Nineteen minutes until boarding.

"All passengers flying to New Delhi must check in now," the agent in front of the gate finally announced. Everyone clamored to line up. An Indian woman and her young son stood in front of me. He tugged on her sleeve.

"Where are we going?" he asked.

"India," she said and kissed him on the head.

"Eeeendeeea," he repeated.

He tugged on her sleeve again.

"Ask me where we are going," he said.

"Where are we going?" she humored him.

"Eeeeendeeeeeaaaahhhh," he sang out with glee.

I boarded the plane and found my window seat next to an old Indian man who looked like a sage character straight out of an ancient text. He had a long white beard, a turban, glasses, and wrinkled hands with long gnarled fingers. His middle-aged son was sitting next to him, and they were having a lively conversation in an Indian-sounding language that I assumed was Hindi.

"Excuse me," I said, and they got up into the aisle so I could get to my seat. I buckled my seatbelt and listened to their indiscernible conversation as I waited for takeoff. I stared out at the rain and the roadway lights dripping down my window.

We'd been sitting on the runway for twenty minutes past the scheduled takeoff time. I was trying to read one of the novels about India I'd brought with me: *The Inheritance of Loss* by Kiran Desai, about a cook in India who sends his son to New York to make a better life. But I just kept re-reading the same line, unable to focus on it at all. I was distracted by my nervousness and the musical discussion to my right. The old man clutched his airplane pillow in his lap as he spoke, then lifted his right hand and fluttered his long fingers every time he made a point. Smooth jazz played low in the background. A baby cried. Finally, the plane started to move. I looked out the window. It had stopped raining. I could make out the Empire State Building in the foggy distance.

I turned on the television screen on the back of the seat in front of me. It flashed "Fourteen hours from destination," then showed a world map with a plane marking where we were and starred New Delhi, where we were headed. I tried to settle into my seat for the long flight and promised myself I would stare at this travel progression screen as little as possible to minimize mental torture. I flipped through the movie selections. *Gandhi* was among them. I'd never seen it before. *Perfect*, I thought. Ten minutes into it, while Gandhi was getting beaten in the stomach with a crowbar, I thought, *This is way too intense for me right now*, and decided to watch a few episodes of *30 Rock*.

I passed the time by watching movies and television, staring at pages of my book, taking multiple trips to the bathroom, doing lunges up and down the aisles, and contorting myself in my seat. I jerked my body from position to position, trying to find one that worked: forehead on the tray table, curled up into a tight fetal lying flat on the seat, head tucked inside the crevice between seat and window, slumped down, legs crossed up in the air.

My private screen flashed, "Four hours and forty minutes from destination." That made it around 3:30 p.m. Delhi time, 6:30 a.m. New York time, 3:30 a.m. San Diego time. In other words, time had been nullified. At this point, both nervousness and excitement were obliterated by my desire for a bed to lie down in. The middle-aged man was standing in the aisle so the old man could sleep stretched out over two seats. He was cramping my leg space, which was making me angry. I dropped my forehead onto the tray table.

Three hours left, two hours, one hour... Finally: "Ladies and gentlemen, we have begun our initial descent into New Delhi. Please put away all electronic devices, and make sure your seat backs and tray tables are in the upright and locked position. The time in New Delhi is 8:30 p.m." Butterflies rushed back through me, flapping madly between my stomach and my throat. I was about to land in India. I cried as the plane landed, grateful for the courage I had to do this all on my own and thrilled that the flight was finally over.

As I walked through the airport, my heart raced with anticipation. Where was I? What was I about to see, learn, discover? The airport felt dilapidated: the walls, floors, and ceilings were all worn out, much different from the immaculate American airports I was used to. I stood in line at customs, vibrating, my mind completely reeling at being in the unknown. I went through health check, assured the lady that I didn't have influenza, had my passport stamped, and made my way to baggage claim. I saw my bag—it was wrapped in plastic; a compartment had busted open during the journey. I made a claim on it and transferred everything from that compartment to the others. As I began to wheel the bag, I realized the wheels had also gotten busted a bit on the journey, so I was part wheeling and part dragging the bag along the ground. My racing heart would not let me worry too much about this problem, as it propelled me to the ATM machine to take out Indian rupees and then through the crowd of cab drivers awaiting new arrivals. They were all clumped behind partitions on either side of the walkway, holding up their signs and yelling out for clients. I imagined I was a queen walking in a parade, and all these people were welcoming me. I found my pre-booked driver holding up his "Amanda Miller" sign and shook his hand. "Hello, ma'am," he said, making excellent eye contact. He was young and had a sweet smile. He part rolled, part dragged my bag for me as we walked outside to the cab.

Outside, it was humid, dark, and polluted. I breathed in the acrid air. We walked past some beaten-up trucks with Hindi writing to get to the cab. The steering wheel was on the right side of the car, like in England. We entertained some driver-passenger banter: *What do you do? What do you like to do for fun? Have you been to India before? Have you been to the States before?* I was impressed by how great his English was and found his accent adorable, thrilled to be having my first conversation with someone from India, in India. I was staring out the window while we spoke, trying to take in every new sight, except there wasn't much to see in the dark and fog, just some street signs in Hindi and cars zooming past. I had been warned about the crazy Indian drivers, and I quickly understood why. There were no designated lanes; the road was a free-for-all. Everyone was driving way too fast and generously honking their horns. My mind was whirling. What was this place? What was going to happen? I had no way of knowing, so all I could do was devote myself entirely to the present moment.

By the time I arrived at the hotel, it was 10:30 p.m. The lobby smelled like must and incense. It was small, with wood-paneled walls and cream tiled floors reflecting fluorescent light. The receptionist was watching the news on a small television at his desk. He had glasses, a tired face, and silver hair, and when he smiled at me, I felt at home. What was it with Indian people and their smiles? I had traveled on my own halfway around the world, and because of those smiles, I didn't feel lonely at all.

"GAP Adventures," I said.

"Yes," he said, "Room 501. Everyone is sleeping. Four forty-five a.m. wakeup call. Five a.m. you leave to go to train station for Jaipur city."

Two nice men lugged my bag up five flights of stairs. I tipped them, closed the door, and flung myself onto the bed. I'd arrived.

No One Wears Shoes Here

My phone rang at 4:45 the next morning, as promised. I hobbled down the stairs, disoriented and jetlagged, falling into the walls with my duffle bag. When I got to the lobby, I met Hari, my local Indian tour guide. He wore a marigold button-down T-shirt tucked into his jeans and two small gold hoop earrings, and had warm dark eyes and a thick mustache that curled up at the edges. After thirteen introductory handshakes with the other group members, Hari ushered us outside into auto rickshaws. It was still dark. The roads were lined with heaps of trash. When we arrived at the train station, I felt my first wave of culture shock. Homeless people were sandwiched together along the entire walkway—male, female, old, young, infants sleeping on cloths on the ground at their mothers' feet. Everyone was coated in dirt and so skinny. It smelled like sewage. I felt goosebumps up the back of my neck. We got down to the platform to wait for the train. An Indian woman's trance-like voice repeated train announcements over the loudspeaker, alternating English and Hindi, with chiming bells between each announcement. My senses were short-circuiting trying to process all the foreign input.

I settled into my seat for the five-hour train ride. As the train chugged along, I looked out the dirty windows at scenery coated in brownish-yellow: expansive green fields, cows, goats, mud huts that looked centuries old. At station platforms, I stared out at crowds of Indian women with nose rings in bright radiant saris and men with ragged button-down shirts and dirt-streaked slacks, all squinting in the sunlight. The train attendant walked up and down the aisles with a big silver thermos, announcing "chai, chai." I asked for some. It was fifteen rupees, the equivalent of thirty cents. As the warm, sweet liquid slid down my throat, my headphones pumped Bob Dylan's "Lily, Rosemary and the Jack of Hearts" into my ears, and I felt euphoric. I was so overcome by the romance of all this, sitting there fantasizing about a life as a travel writer—articles with a personal slant. All this previously unimaginable sensory input nullified my routine thought patterns. I was not mulling over the past or panicking about the future. I was sitting on a train in completely foreign territory, surrounded by strangers, and I was undeniably happy. I wanted to hold onto this feeling forever.

I opened up my GAP Adventures India travel guide. On the first page, there was a heading, "The Right to Develop." Beneath, it talked about how visiting westerners should keep in mind that while India does not have the material wealth of western countries, it is rich with spirituality and community, which are often lacking in the first world. I leaned back in my seat and closed my eyes, trying to imagine an America rich with spirituality and community. It seemed to contradict the defining American principles: survival of the fittest and manifest destiny. I dozed off and dreamt about growing up in a mud hut without a mall in sight.

When we got off the train in Jaipur, child beggars swarmed around us. These little people with dirty faces, ragged clothing, and bare feet went from person to person, tugging on our clothes, reaching their palms out, and bringing their hands to their mouths. "Hello, ma'am, money, ma'am, please." My euphoria was immediately trumped by pangs of guilt about my comparative good fortune. I berated myself for all the time I had spent being unhappy when I had my health, clothing, shelter, and food. Meanwhile, these children, who should have been in school learning how to write their names, were begging for money for food and didn't even have shoes. I wanted to empty my wallet into their calloused bony hands and go find something sharp and steel with which to impale myself for my ingratitude. As I reached into my pocket for some change to give, the least I could do to console myself, Hari stopped me. "Don't give anything to anyone," he said, "It will just encourage others to come up and beg from you. You can't give to everyone, so just look away." At first I was stunned by how cold it seemed, but it made sense; I couldn't give to everyone.

As we waited while he bargained fares to our hotel with a nearby crew of rickshaw drivers, the group of children continued to weave through us, begging. I found it almost impossible not to stare at those young wide-eyed faces. Two little girls hooked onto my sympathetic gaze and teamed up on me, one tugging at the back of my shirt, one tugging at my pants. "Hello, ma'am, money, ma'am. Please, ma'am," they squeaked. I closed my eyes and grew very still, like I would if bees were swarming around me. *I am lucky, I am lucky, I am lucky*, I repeated in my head. The girls smelled like dirt and sweat. I opened my eyes and looked down at the one in front of me. She pointed to my water bottle. "You want this?" I asked, lifting it up. She nodded her head yes, and when I gave it to her, she flashed one of the biggest smiles I had ever seen. Just then, Hari called to us to come load our baggage on top of the rickshaws. I rushed over, climbed on, and didn't look back, still repeating *I am lucky* to myself. It was like a revelation; why didn't I know how lucky I was before?

The ride to the hotel was an extreme roller coaster for the senses. I felt like I had stepped out of a time machine; this place seemed centuries old. There were crazy rickshaw drivers, incessant honking horns, no lanes, cows wandering the streets, bright colors, the smell of cow feces mingling with burning incense. A mother stood beside her small toddler, naked from the waist down, sitting in the middle of the road. A fully nude child held his father's hand crossing the street. Women in saris. Sun-worn faces. Oppressive heat. Streets lined with mud, dirt, trash, animal shit, urine, crumbling buildings. Camels, pigs, dogs, elephants, cows. This was all real—just another place where people lived, except everything was different. As I took in all the sights, sounds, and smells, I forgot to think about myself; it was an incredible relief.

As the tour proceeded, I welcomed my ego's temporary leave of absence. I was really in the moment, enjoying getting to know the people in my group from Switzerland, Denmark, Lithuania, Canada, England, Scotland, Spain, Australia, and South Africa as much as I enjoyed being surprised every day by what I saw and experienced in India. We toured palaces and temples, sat for long delicious meals of curries and naan bread, stared out train windows, wandered the streets, fended off beggars, and bargained in marketplaces. We battled squat toilets and brushed our teeth with bottled water.

We took way too many photos of the Taj Mahal, a place I couldn't actually process being near; it was massive and stunning, and it may as well have been a mirage. After we'd exhausted ourselves taking photos of the palace, we sat down near the fountain in front. Indian tourists stared at us and we stared back, equally fascinated by these foreign human beings. Soon they approached and asked if they could have their picture taken with us. We obliged and asked the same in return. We continued this back and forth for a while. I found it quite amusing that this was happening in front of the great Taj Mahal. Feeling happy and lucky, I couldn't understand how I had ever felt otherwise.

My twenty-sixth birthday was the next day. That morning, we were going to a nice hotel near ours for a huge buffet breakfast before our seven-hour train ride to the small town of Orchha. I was a little late getting to the lobby. I scurried down the three flights of stairs to find Hari waiting alone. "Happy birthday!" he exclaimed and gave me a big hug.

"Where is everyone?" I asked.

"Already at breakfast. Let's go."

We walked four blocks past honking cars and rickshaws, trash, and the local tourist Pizza Hut to the hotel and down the stairs to the restaurant.

"Happy birthday!" exclaimed my thirteen tour mates in unison, seated around the long table.

I sat down, and a waiter set a round gooey chocolate cake with candles in front of me. Everyone sang "Happy Birthday." I blew out my candles and wished for inner peace.

On the train to Orchha, Hari sat down next to me as I was writing in my journal. I felt him staring at me for a while before he spoke.

"Are you an artist?" he asked, playing with his mustache.

"A writer."

"What do you write? Novels?"

"I write about personal experiences."

"Are you honest?"

"Yes."

I looked out the train window for several minutes, and Hari asked me, "What are you thinking about?"

"Nothing, just looking."

"Really? Your mind is totally blank?"

"Just thinking about how cool it is to be here, trying to process it all. Traveling is really good for relaxing the mind. Nothing is familiar. I don't have a phone. I'm not checking e-mail. I'm not worrying about anything. Just being."

"That's how I feel when I go to my farm," he said. "Totally content and at peace."

"It's so nice to feel content, isn't it?" I said. "It's relieving."

"Yeah, people are never satisfied with what they have. They always want more."

No kidding. I certainly had the "it's never enough" disease. I could never live up to my own impossible standards. I'd always wanted to do more, accomplish more, especially as an actor and a writer. I wanted these things so deeply and in such a desperate painful way. Why couldn't I just pursue them with grace and ease? Why did the desire have to torture me incessantly? As I thought about this, I felt tremors threatening my contented state, ironic as we sat there talking about contentment. I didn't want to have this conversation anymore. I hadn't thought about these things in nearly a week and didn't want to blow my peace. My gaze drifted toward the window, which displayed a woman with a basket on her head.

"Do you have a boyfriend?" Hari asked me.

"No. What about you? Are you married? Any kids?"

"I have two sons. I was married, but I'm not anymore. It was an arranged marriage. That's how it works in India. I was lonely, so I thought I'd get married and all my problems would be solved, being with someone who was assigned to love me. But it didn't work out. It was never good. We got a divorce, which is very frowned upon in India. But sometimes you have to make hard choices in life, change what's happening if it's not what you want so you find what you want."

"But still, you had two children together."

"Yes," he said and raised his eyebrows, "thanks to rum."

Hari got up to go to the bathroom as my mind echoed, *Change what's happening if it's not what you want so you can find what you want.* I closed my eyes and continued to fixate on this phrase until it disintegrated into meaningless vowels and consonants. Suddenly, the train stopped. We'd arrived in Orchha. When did that happen? Hari was sitting next to me reading a newspaper. I hadn't remembered him returning. I had apparently just emerged from a staring time warp. I picked up my bag and walked into Hari.

"Are you okay?" he asked.

"Yeah, totally."

Find what you want. Find what you want. Change what's happening…

Several hours later, we arrived at our resort with air-conditioned tents, a pool, and massage services on the edge of the small poverty-stricken town of Orchha. At first I felt extremely guilty about our accommodations but then convinced myself to transform guilt into gratitude. I decided to give myself a birthday present in the form of an Ayurvedic massage, familiar with this type of massage from an introductory lecture during my massage training at The School of Healing Arts. But that was the extent of my knowledge, and I was excited to receive one in its country of origin. I also thought that maybe a massage would bring my mind back to its contented state, as it seemed to be slipping.

This was a much different kind of massage experience from what I was used to giving and receiving back home. I entered the room and shook my female therapist's hand. There was no soft music, no dim lighting, just a massage table in the middle of a white-walled room with white tiled floors. The therapist instructed me to remove my clothing, and I waited for her to leave the room to respect my modesty, but after an awkwardly long pause where she continued to stare at me, I realized she wasn't going anywhere. I felt uncomfortable taking off all my clothes in front of her, but chalked it up to cultural difference and disrobed. I assumed I was supposed to lie down on the table, but she motioned that I should first sit in the plastic chair she stood beside. I obliged and sat my bare ass down on the toweled chair while she poured oil all over my head and gave me a head massage.

This woman was very clinical, unthreatening, and barely spoke English. Nevertheless, my feelings about my body were raw; I felt exposed and nervous, like when I was naked in front of a man, the only other times I'd ever let anyone see me without clothes. At those times, I generally tried to detach from my nakedness; as long as I didn't look down at myself, I was as good as covered. But this never worked; I felt very vulnerable, subject to fierce scrutiny, mainly my own. I felt the parts of my body that remained hidden were hidden for good reason. I hated my breasts: the left visibly larger than the right, replete with stretch marks, not perky, with small nipples, one almost always inverted. Despite my overall thin physique, I'd never had a flat stomach and was embarrassed by its pudginess. I could never bring myself to get a Brazilian wax and was self-conscious about my pubic hair.

Generally with men, the lights were low whenever I was naked, and I made sure to cover myself as soon as the sex acts were through. But there I was in this Indian massage room, plopped down naked in front of an unfamiliar set of eyes in the light of day. I shut my eyes tightly, felt the air against my skin, and tried to allow the fingers digging into my scalp to feel good. But I found it impossible to relax.

After several long minutes, she tapped me on the shoulder and motioned for me to lie down on the table. Thank God. I took hurried steps to get there and was relieved to be able to lie on my stomach. She poured oil all over me, and applied swift and generous strokes across my back. I closed my eyes. After several deep breaths and the safety of being on my belly, I was miraculously able to transcend my nakedness. The strokes felt good, and I disappeared into that blessed meditative massage state, falling deep into the black cushions in front of my eyes...until it was time to turn over. Once I was on my back, I was incapable of re-entering the meditative realm. I told her I was cold and asked for a towel. She obliged. But I still couldn't relax as I lay there, cursing my physical inadequacies.

Afterward, instead of feeling calm and refreshed as I had hoped, I felt more disgruntled and insecure, rushing to put my clothes back on and hiding in my room until I relaxed enough to face the group. When I finally emerged, everyone was eating samosas and pakoras, getting drunk by the pool. I sat with them and was polite when spoken to, but didn't eat, drink, or speak much.

Later that evening, we visited an outdoor Hindu temple in town for a prayer service. It was now several hours later, and I had basically recovered from my afternoon trauma. I was looking forward to the service, hoping it would transport me somewhere deep and spiritual. We had to take off our shoes before entering. But when we went in, there were these little beetles everywhere that crawled all over our feet, flew into our hair and onto our clothes, covering us all over. The local people were all clustered in front of an altar with statues of Hindu gods, chanting and prostrating themselves, paying no mind to the fact that they, too, were cloaked in beetles. I was trying to be respectful and get into the zone, but along with the rest of my tour mates, all I could concentrate on was swatting the beetles or kicking them off my feet. When we left the temple, local kids swarmed us, trying to sell us trinkets. When we said, "No, thank you," they followed us and persisted. I was unsympathetic; I wanted to swat at them as I had the beetles. This birthday had started out so promising, and it seemed to have gone awry.

At the end of the day, I lay on my bed feeling depressed, lonely, and deflated. Where had all the magic gone? The novelty of the group was wearing off, and I was tired of making conversation all day. I wanted to be with a loved one and not a huge group of strangers. Also, the newness of the adventure was already fading, and I was starting to think about my life again; these blasted routine thought patterns always re-emerged regardless of circumstance. I begged my mind to please let me keep enjoying myself and slipped into a restless sleep. I had violent sex dreams all night long: incoherent flashes of being punched in the face repeatedly, having a knife dragged across the surface of my torso, and being penetrated so roughly it hurt, the man's body slamming against mine, knocking the wind out of me.

The next night, we took a thirteen-hour night train to Varanasi. On the way, I read about the city in my travel book. Varanasi is a holy city in Hinduism, one of the religion's most sacred pilgrimage sites. The city is built along the Ganges River, which is believed to be a highly auspicious place; pilgrims travel from all over the world to bathe in its water. People also believe that if they die in Varanasi, they will be ultimately freed from the cycle of rebirth. There are crematoriums all along the river for dead bodies to be burned and the ashes scattered throughout the water. I was intrigued by the intensity and couldn't wait to get there. I wanted to be shocked as a way of being jolted out of myself.

We woke up at 5 a.m. the next morning to board bicycle rickshaws to the Ganges River for a morning boat ride. I felt so bad for my driver; he was a small man and looked like he was struggling so much, pulling two people's weight along the potholed roads. We arrived at the shore of the alarmingly dirty river: thick brown with all kinds of disgusting debris floating in it, definitely a hotbed for disease. We watched people bathe in that disgusting water. Men dunked their babies under the murky surface. I saw a man climb out of the river wearing only a small cloth over his lower half, sit up on a rock in a cross-legged meditative pose, close his eyes, and begin some intensive breathing exercises. I stared at his protruding ribs, and watched him pump his abdomen in and out with every fast breath. The faith was fierce and palpable, and made me shiver.

We drifted past a floating partially decomposed cow carcass. Then we passed a floating human corpse, and I almost vomited. Our tour guide Hari informed us that sometimes people just throw the bodies into the river if they cannot afford the cremation ceremony.

We took the boat to the shore, where we exited, and Hari led us along the banks of the Ganges. Passing the crematorium, we watched a body being prepared for cremation. The body was elevated on a platform with men standing on either end; it reminded me of a skewered chicken. There was a giant pile of ashes on the ground below the body. The wind blew ashes into our hair. Mud-caked rabid dogs circled our feet, their coats torn, leaving patches of dried blood. I prayed I wouldn't be bitten.

We passed two men sitting on the steps wearing holy saffron gowns. One of them had dreadlocked hair, and his skin was covered in what appeared to be a white powder. "That's not powder, " Hari said. "That's ashes of dead bodies. These men are called Sadhus."

He went on to explain that Sadhus were wandering ascetics, people who had renounced everything in search of enlightenment. They normally wandered around naked or with just a thin loincloth but were wearing robes out of respect for their proximity to the holy river. They smoked hashish and took other hallucinogenic substances totally sanctioned by the government, as they were for spiritual purposes. Sadhus would even go so far as to drink their own urine and eat pieces of dead bodies to prove their austerity. I didn't understand who decided that these were the ways to prove one's devotion to the Lord.

I felt both physically repulsed and morbidly seduced by the whole scene. The effect was deep and primal. I wanted things to just keep shocking me until I dissolved inside the shock, forgetting myself, my confusions, my cravings, my life. As I stared back at the body being prepared for cremation, I fantasized about being beaten, violently raped, cut and tortured. There was this angry, pained aggressive beast writhing inside me that desperately craved volcanic orgasm, an explosive convergence of pleasure and pain. I closed my eyes, took a deep breath of burnt flesh, opened my eyes, and smiled at my tour mates as we walked along. I wondered what was going on behind their polite grins.

I was sitting in the back of a parked bicycle rickshaw, waiting to leave the Ganges, when a woman approached me. With her dirty face and sari, holding a dirty sleeping baby naked from the waist down, she looked me in the eye, extended her cupped palm toward me for money, then raised her hand to her mouth. I could see sores on her baby's legs. Then she reached her hand toward me and pulled at my sleeve, reached her hand back up to her mouth, pointed to the baby, and lifted up his shirt to show me his skeletal frame. Crying and muttering unintelligibly, she grabbed my sleeve again, yanking this time, hand back up to her mouth, desperate. It was thirty seconds extending into eternity, and I sat paralyzed.

I tried not to look at her and her child, but was incapable of not looking. I stared at them, unable to fully process that she was real, her baby was real, India was real. This all existed in the same time continuum as New York City, as the United States.

I held my breath, tensed every muscle in my body. She continued yanking on my sleeve, crying, muttering. The baby's head hung off his neck unsupported. Just when I felt like my heart might really explode, shooting all my fleshy bits out across the city of Varanasi, the rickshaw pulled away, and I left her standing there. She disappeared behind the torrent of buses, rickshaws, cars, dust clouds, cows, cow shit, goats, pedestrians, flies, women sitting sideways on the backs of motorcycles—bright saris flapping and flying, honking horns. No one wears shoes here.

That night I dreamt about being brutally raped. The dream was so visceral: The man had blindfolded me so I could not see his face, but I felt his weight crushing me. I woke up in the middle of the night, sweating, with severe stomach pain. I flopped around in my bed, clutching my abdomen, and got up several times to dry heave and shit liquid. When I fell back asleep, I dreamt about being dragged across a bed of nails.

At 5 a.m. the next morning, feeling twitchy and exhausted, I boarded a bus with the word "Tourist" splayed across the top of the windshield. The ride from Varanasi, India, to Lumbini, Nepal (the birthplace of Buddha), would take twelve hours. We passed heaps of muddy garbage, goats and cows, handmade huts, laundry hanging out to dry, dirty men in rags with sores on their legs, defecating beside cows defecating. As the bus bumped down the pot-holed road, the girls behind me whined, "I'm going to be sick," and then the girls behind them, "Turn off the air conditioning!" So the air went off; suddenly it was stuffy and smelled like rotten bananas and human feces.

Meanwhile, all my desires were crawling through me alongside the crawling scenery: *I want to publish a book, perform a solo show, find love.* These wants felt like twisting knives in my heart, so intense. Why was it so painful to want these things? And why were these desires attacking me then and there?

I looked out the window at two small children walking nearby, an older brother holding his younger sister's hand, both of them laughing. She was wearing her hair in pigtails, like I used to at her age. But she was not wearing shoes, and her clothes were tattered and torn. Her smile beamed. I dug my nails into my forearms. *I am lucky*, I reminded myself. But my desires didn't care; I felt them wrapping their fingers around my neck.

I leaned my head against the window and thought about how I'd signed up to sponsor a child in India. Two weeks before my departure, after buying my plane ticket and booking the tour, I had gotten off work and didn't feel like going home yet, so I sat on a curb in Union Square to meditate on the flurry of frantic pedestrians. There was a man standing in front of me in a blue Children's International T-shirt. He was doing the normal guerilla street marketing: "Do you have a minute for the children?" Of course, no one had a minute. I was sympathetic to the passersby; I don't usually like being attacked by people and their causes when I am rushing somewhere. After fifteen minutes of watching that guy get rejected, I called out to him, "Hey, I have a minute for the children, tell me about them." I knew I had done myself in.

He sat down beside me on the curb and pulled out his binder, flipping through pictures of skinny smiling children from impoverished countries.

"For twenty-two dollars a month, this child can receive health care and go to school. Come on," he said, "how much money do you just drop on a night out?"

I had emptied my bank account, cashed all the bonds I'd saved from relatives since childhood, and accepted a generous financial contribution from my mother, spending thousands of dollars to travel to a place where people were struggling to meet their basic needs. I was quitting my job and uncertain about my financial future, but come on, just twenty-two dollars a month. Later that week, I received my welcome packet with a photo of Bikash Kayal, age nine. He speaks Bengali and enjoys studying languages, playing with friends, and drawing.

With my head still against the window, I squeezed my eyes shut and repeated, *I am lucky*, as my cravings continued to slither relentlessly inside my skin: head to neck to shoulders, torso, hips, knees, toes, like a snake sliding up and down, down and up, hissing, *I want to be an accomplished writer and performer. I want to feel a man's fingertips trail my body while he kisses my knuckles and tell me how beautiful I am, how soft my skin is, how he can't imagine life without me.*

Staring out the window of the bus with trash, shit, and crumbling structures everywhere, I prayed for self-actualization. That was my ultimate craving. *May I work toward my goals with peace and grace, may the pain from these desires cease.*

Buddha said suffering is caused by craving, and he preached the middle way: Become master over your cravings, and you will reach nirvana.

I shut my eyes. My head bumped as the bus bumped. "Get some sleep," some voice from somewhere whispered. "The rocket will be at your door before sunrise to shoot you straight up to heaven."

When we arrived at Hotel Nirvana in Lumbini, I wanted to be alone. I excused myself from the group and went up to my room. I sat quietly on the bed, looking out the window at dark green trees and mountains and their silhouettes, clouds pink from the setting sun. What was I doing? How was wandering around India any different from the wandering I'd been doing in my life? Who was I? What did I ultimately want? I felt achingly lonely. I shut the curtains and lay down on top of the bed, closed my eyes, and slid my right hand down my pants. *Strong, productive me, I can take on the world.* I tilted my head back while moving my middle finger in slow circles. *I can travel to foreign places all alone. I'm not afraid.* I sped up the movements, squeezed my eyelids together, clenched my jaw. *I can work hard. I can accomplish anything.* I bit my lower lip, moving my finger faster up and down. *I am independent, I am strong, I am unstoppable.* I squeezed my left fist, clenched my jaw, lifted my hips, moved my finger faster. *I am worthy, I am alive, I am, I am, I am, I am, I am.* I lowered my hips, released my jaw, sank my head into the pillow, and dragged my right hand out from under my pants, resting it on my abdomen. My limp hand rose and fell against my slow, deep breaths.

Directing my closed eyes to the point between my eyebrows, under the influence of the surrounding spiritual landscape, I blessed my future love. I didn't know where he was or what he looked like. But I believed in him, in us, in our future together.

Our next stop was Chitwan National Park, a majestic getaway surrounded by wide green fields, jungles, lakes, and distant mountains. The air smelled like fresh grass, and with a light breeze, the temperature was simply perfect. It seemed the more beautiful the landscape, the further I slid into a pool of melancholic contemplation. I was becoming increasingly internal, and though I made polite conversation with my tour mates and laughed at their jokes, I was often somewhere else entirely, trying to devise a plan for my future. I was becoming particularly consumed by a longing to perform. It had been nearly five years since I had been immersed in theater; for so long, it had been what made me feel most alive and ignited. Since my breakdown, I had not returned to it with the same intensity. I also passionately wanted to finish and publish my memoir. How was I going to support myself when I got back to New York? How could I best set myself up for success? While bike riding through the jungle and riding an elephant seemed to be great opportunities for tour group bonding, these activities only sank me to deeper levels of introspection. I felt unable to relate to anyone, overwhelmed by a profound sense of loneliness.

Amanda Erin Miller

When we got back to our hotel, I sat on the porch in front of my room. I wiped the tears off my face as I wrote in my journal:

I'll be your parent. I'll breathe into the tight sore spots, cry as much and as often as necessary. I'll rock you until you fall asleep. I'll catch you when you start beating yourself. I promise to always believe in you, cheer you on, and respect you when you need to sit quietly, not berate you for being reclusive. There is such a thing as healthy solitude, and I'm here to help you nurture that.

"*Namaste*," greeted the resort attendant, startling me as she turned on the porch light for me to write by.

"*Namaste* and thank you," I replied, disoriented by the gap between internal and external worlds.

This trip with its mind-blowing sites and life-altering experiences was entirely solipsistic. As much as I intended to relay events to friends and family through words and images when I returned, no one would ever be able comprehend what it felt like to be there. I looked up at the black sky: bright half moon, millions of stars. I closed my eyes and imagined being held by my love, our bodies warm up against each other between the sheets with moonlight streaming through the window. I imagined him kissing my face and neck, running his fingers through my hair. The thought gave me goosebumps. I let my eyelids lift very slowly, allowing the light to creep in bit by bit. Then I looked back up at the sky and down at my journal, where I continued to drag my pen across the page:

I opened the door for Blue. He was standing there holding a bouquet of blue roses. I was in the middle of cleaning my apartment. He held out his hand and I, such a sucker for him, dropped everything and grabbed on tightly. We walked for at least three miles under the stars before I started to get suspicious, stopped, and asked, "Where are you taking me?"

"To dance."

"How far is it?"

"Not too far. We just have to wade through the river, hitch a ride on an elephant, catch a Jeep, ride a bike through the jungle, and climb to the top of a mountain. When we get there, I promise there will be a band playing beautiful romantic melodies, and we will dance."

I stopped and thought for a minute. It seemed like a lot of work for a simple dance with Blue. I had dishes in the sink, and my roommate would be home any minute. Plus, all that activity and I hadn't even eaten dinner yet.

"Blue, can I ask you a question?"

"Of course," he said, gently moving the hair out of my face.

"Where is this going?"

He took a step away from me and closed his eyes.

I closed mine, too, and listened to my breath, the crickets, the rustling of leaves.

The blackness behind my closed lids began to morph and swirl into different shades and textures. The swirls became ocean waves crashing dark blue against a blue-black sky. The waves funneled into a whirlpool as the sky released monsoon rain. Then it all swirled back together into two twisting spirals, one in front of each eye—all different shades of blue. The blue began to morph into purple, green, orange until all I could see was bright sun yellow. I opened my eyes, and Blue was gone. I got down on my knees and stared at the grassy spot where he'd been standing. I lowered my forehead to that spot and stretched my arms out on the ground in front of my head, palms facing down, fingers spread wide.

"I'm sorry, Blue," I muttered, and then slowly stood up. After taking a quick look at the starry sky, I turned to go back home and finish my dishes.

I rested my head against the wall behind me, listening to the chirping crickets and the rustling of leaves. Then I closed my journal, put it away in my room, and went to meet the rest of the group for dinner.

During the six-hour bus ride to Pokhara, our next stop, I was really struggling to stay present. My mind was flooded with anxiety about my lack of a future plan. I berated my brain for distracting me with such a useless thought in the midst of this beautiful lakeside village surrounded by mountains. After dropping off my bags at the hotel, I walked down the main road with two British girls from my group, listening to Tibetan chants and going from store to store, examining magnificent scarves, paintings, and incense. Yet I continued to be distracted and disgruntled: I wanted to make $2,000 a month to support myself in New York City and devote myself to writing and performing. Would I be able to accomplish this? I fought against these thoughts, knowing that if I could not get myself to stay present for this once-in-a-lifetime experience, I would absolutely regret it. *Relax, brain. Listen to the birds, smell the fresh air, breathe it all in.*

We were in Pokhara for two nights before white water rafting for part of the journey from Pokhara to Kathmandu. It was my first time whitewater rafting, and the setting was truly idyllic. We floated down the shimmering blue river, surrounded by green mountains. The water glistened under the sun. Floating down that river surrounded by such sublime natural beauty jolted me back to the present; my thoughts all melted and dissolved into the river. We stopped for lunch at a sandy bank with rocks and streams. The sand was white and glistened. Everyone's face glistened. Our three Nepali guides prepared lunch for us: a batch of fresh coleslaw, soft sliced bread, peanut butter and jelly, biscuits and tuna salad. The lunch glistened. I felt like I was in a trance as I ate my lunch silently with my back against a rock, listening to the rush of the river's current.

Kathmandu was the last stop on the tour. It was a crowded city, and so polluted that my throat hurt by the end of my first day there. We spent one day and one night together as a group, visiting a Buddhist temple on a hill and wandering around the city. Hari left the next morning, while the rest of us hung around together for one more afternoon and night. Some people were returning home, while others were continuing to travel on their own or with guided tours to such places as Thailand, Tibet, and China, or to trek in the mountains surrounding Kathmandu. We all went out for a Tibetan dinner on our last night together as a group, and I realized that after two weeks of spending all day every day with these people, I had actually grown comfortable around them. We had experienced so much together, things to which nobody else in our home lives would be able to relate, and suddenly it was time for us to part. Throughout dinner, I was feeling a mounting separation anxiety, as the next phase of my trip would be traveling to Mumbai and then the ashram by myself, which made me insanely nervous.

Traveling alone was extremely stressful from the start. The night before my departure, I was sitting in my hotel lobby and saw a headline splayed across the front page of the newspaper, *Jet Airways Strike Continues*. Both my flights were on Jet Airways. What if my flights were cancelled? I felt the anxiety building in my chest.

Luckily, my flight was not cancelled, but I was still all wound up. I flew to Delhi, where I planned to get a connecting flight to Mumbai. My first stop was the currency exchange counter. I had 7,000 Nepali rupees in my money belt, the equivalent of 100 U.S. dollars. The man would not change it for me. He told me that India had no interest in Nepali rupees. I nearly punched him in the face. Then I missed my connecting flight from Delhi to Mumbai, and panic set in. But it really wasn't that big of a deal; I just got a ticket for the next flight an hour later. As I left the ticket counter with clenched fists, wanting to pound my thighs with my knuckles, I pleaded with myself to pull it together.

I was really hungry and didn't have any cash, so I went to the ATM. My ATM card didn't work. I tried it again. It still didn't work. I wanted to gouge my eyes out. A lady sitting nearby saw how worked up I was getting and pointed out that the ATM was for Visa cards only. Mine was Mastercard. I shook my head and again reminded myself to chill out. Then I went to an ATM that said "Mastercard." It still didn't work.

"Motherfucker!" I shouted and kicked the machine. How was I going to get something to eat? My ATM card had been unpredictably selective about the machines it would work for throughout the trip. And it usually sent me into a rage. Now, I was going to have to cash one of my traveler's checks, which was meant to pay for the yoga program.

Worked up, sweating, hungry, with anxiety plastered across my face, I approached the currency exchange desk. The Indian gentleman was breezily humming a Hindi tune. What nerve.

"I need to cash a U.S. traveler's check," I panted.

"Okay, no problem," he said and continued to hum. He took out the paperwork, wrote slowly, and hummed some more. Meanwhile, I felt my heart racing and resented how peaceful he was. "Enjoy your life, without worry," he said and handed me my cash. At first the comment made me angry, like when people tell me to smile when I'm in a bad mood. Then I wanted to jump over the counter and hug him. I realized how ridiculous it was to resent someone for being peaceful just because I was a ball of angst. *Amanda, pull yourself together. Have patience, be flexible, and stop stressing so much about things you can't control.* After getting the money, I stuffed my face with pizza and ice cream to comfort myself, thinking, *Ashram, here comes an American stress case, I hope you're ready.*

By the time I got to my hotel in Mumbai, it was dark. I'd found a budget hotel in my *Lonely Planet* guidebook for thirty-six dollars a night that included air conditioning. My room was hideous, with awful fluorescent lighting, dirty white walls with paint peeling all over the place, a mattress, and pillows as hard as rocks. I didn't feel entirely safe, as there was just one man and myself staying on my floor. I had already determined he was a rapist and serial killer. But I was hungry again, so I ventured out to find some food.

There was a crew of men gathered around a car on the dark street outside my hotel. They flocked toward me. "Hello, ma'am," they echoed, a broken chorus. "Yes, ma'am, you want to go somewhere? You looking for something?" I was clearly a confused-looking white girl all alone. I felt like I was asking to be murdered.

I was able to skirt past them on my mission for food. I went into the first restaurant on the main street: Lebanese. I got a vegetarian wrap to go and took it back with me, avoiding eye contact with the same mob, nearly hyperventilating as I rushed past. When I returned to the hotel, I locked myself in my room and decided there would be no sightseeing in Mumbai. I would leave first thing in the morning to fly into the ashram's open arms. I had full confidence the ashram was going to save me from myself.

Things didn't seem quite as scary in the daylight. I called for my complimentary breakfast of tea and two slices of bread with butter. The Indian man who delivered the food to my door was very sweet. He had a young face, a warm smile, and adorable dimpled cheeks. I wanted to embrace him and lean my head on his shoulder, but I shook his hand instead.

"What country are you from, madam?" he asked.

"The USA."

"United States of America. Very good country. Obama president. I like him. Very good politician. Things changing over there, yes?"

"Yes, definitely."

He looked down at my giant piece of luggage, looked up, and flashed a grin.

"Very big bag. When you ready to check out, call me, and I'll take it down to reception for you."

"Thank you."

I closed the door behind him, sat at the window, and enjoyed my toast and tea in the company of chirping birds and honking horns. Good morning, Mumbai.

Reinvigorated by travel romance, I decided to go for a brief wander before heading to the train station. But I forgot to check the train schedule, so I ended up having to wait at the station for four hours for the next train to Nasik. Seething with rage in the oppressive mid-morning heat, I plopped myself down on my duffle bag in front of the station and took out my journal, scribbling violently as crowds bustled in and out of the entrance and parked taxi drivers hollered at passersby. I'd been sitting for just a few minutes when an Indian man approached me, leaning his sweaty face toward mine.

"You have ticket?" he asked. His breath reeked of onion, and I could smell his foul body odor.

"Yes," I said, tensing my jaw, not looking up from my journal.

He breathed heavily in my face for a moment then scurried away.

My reprieve was short-lived. Minutes later, another man approached me.

"Bus to Goa?" he asked.

"No."

He also lingered for an uncomfortable moment, then walked off, only to soon be replaced by another man.

"You need taxi, madam? You want Mumbai tour? Five hundred rupees for the day."

"No, leave me alone."

I stashed my journal in my bag, lunged past him, and lugged my bag back into the ticketing office, where I was able to sit on a bench and wait out the remaining time free of harassment. With the help of Salmon Rushdie's *Midnight's Children,* Bob Dylan, and my own journal ramblings, the hours ultimately passed, the train finally came, the four hours on the train passed, and at long last I arrived in Nasik.

I got an auto-rickshaw to take me from the Nasik station to the ashram's city office, where I would check in and get a taxi to the actual ashram. The rickshaw slammed into the back of a car on the way. My neck lurched backward, and I bit my tongue.

When I arrived at the office, shaken and praying I didn't have whiplash, I was greeted by two Indian men. They informed me that I would have to wait a while to get a taxi. I dropped off my luggage and decided to walk around on the nearby city streets to find a phone to call my mother and tell her I had arrived safely. I was feeling especially anxious after the accident and more stressed about not knowing where I was. All I wanted was to hear my mother's voice, and I would feel better.

I was walking around a nearby street and couldn't find an international phone to use. I kept asking people; nobody spoke English. People kept pointing in contradicting directions until I was walking up and down the street, in and out of stores, and felt like screaming. I returned to a cell phone shop I had visited earlier with a man who did speak English and started crying when I asked him for help again finding a phone.

"What happened? Don't cry," he said. "People will think I did something to you."

"All I want to do is call my mom," I blubbered, snot running.

He walked me down to a phone a few shops away. I called my mom and she answered.

"I arrived at the office in Nasik. I'm safe."

"Good! It's great to hear your voice. Thank you for calling. I love you."

"I love you, too."

I hung up and felt much better until I realized it was dark out and I couldn't remember how to get back to the ashram's office. A new panic set in. I didn't want to get lost wandering the back streets in the dark, so I returned to my friend at the cell phone shop to ask for help getting back to the office. He started to give me directions, but I couldn't follow them.

Finally, he asked, "Do you want me to drop you off?"

I took one second to examine my intuition and said, "Yes, please." He walked me out to his motorcycle in the parking lot. *Oh, God, please don't make this the worst decision of my life.* We got on the bike, no helmets; I held on to him. It was my first time ever on a motorcycle, and I'd never realized how fast those things could go. I was terrified by the speed. I squeezed this stranger's waist, closed my eyes, and prayed. Minutes later, I arrived safely at the office. He smiled generously and sped off. *Thank you, guardian angel.*

Hari Om

By the time I arrived at the ashram, I was a complete basket case. I just wanted to take a shower and go to sleep. A volunteer greeted me upon arrival and directed me to my provisional room.

"Can I take a shower?" I asked her.

"Yes, there are showers, but they are cold. If you want hot water, it comes out of the faucet into a bucket, and you can pour it over yourself that way."

"Okay, uh, thanks," I said, surprised, deciding not to shower that night.

"If you need anything, I'm right next door. You'll hear the bell at 5 a.m., but you don't have to get up yet. That's just because there's another course going on. Breakfast is at 9 a.m. There will be another bell then. Sleep well."

"Thanks," I said before entering the room and absorbing the shock. The walls were a faded light blue, crumbling in places. There were four beds, each surrounded by a curtain. The beds had the thinnest mattresses I had ever seen atop wooden planks, with metal rods poking up from each corner to support mosquito netting. The sheets were like old thin tablecloths. I lay down on a bed and could feel my hipbone digging through the mattress into the wood plank. I couldn't believe I was really going to have to sleep on that bed for a month. Dead beetles were scattered along the windowpane.

There were two documents against the wall by each bed. One was titled, "What Is an Ashram?" and the other, "Code of Conduct in the Ashram." In "What Is an Ashram?" one of the lines read, "An ashram is designed for simplicity. The ashram gives us what we need and not what we want." Clearly that included rock-hard beds. I *needed* somewhere to lie down and sleep that was not the ground. I *wanted* a comfortable mattress. Then I thought I would *need* to do yoga every day to get the kinks out of my back and neck after sleeping on that plank every night. Also, cold-water showers only. Need: to wash myself. Want: hot water. I wondered what other need/want situations were lurking around the corner. I fell asleep knowing this was a place where I wouldn't be able to hide from myself. There would be nowhere to go and no distractions; I thought it was important for me to learn to deal with my bare self in this way.

I woke to the sound of the breakfast bell at 9:00 am, as predicted. My body ached from the hard mattress. I stepped outside into the light and nearly fell over as I caught my first glimpse of the ashram's sublime surroundings: lush green fields and breathtaking distant mountains. The sky was bright blue and cloudless; everything seemed to sparkle in the sunlight. I breathed in the clean air and walked down the hill for my first meal.

The meals were all strictly vegetarian and served buffet style. There were white plastic tables and chairs surrounding a floor area lined with cloth where people could sit cross-legged and dine. I lined up to get my tin dishes and retrieve food from large pots. All meals were to be eaten in silence. This forced us to focus entirely on the food we were eating, the fact that it was nourishing us and keeping us alive. There was a sign on the wall that said, "Shh, be silent. Encourage your inner peace." There was another beside it that said, "For optimum digestion, chew each mouthful thirty-two times." I certainly did not have the discipline to take it that far.

Another teacher-training program had already been going on for two weeks, overlapping with mine, which was scheduled to begin the following morning. As I chewed my saffron rice with potatoes and vegetables, I looked around me at the veteran group and felt intimidated. Everyone seemed really serious. Some people closed their eyes and prayed before eating. Some closed their eyes while chewing. One guy was wearing a sign that said, "I am in silence today." Several people were sporting red bindis on their foreheads and prayer beads around their necks. I wondered what kind of cult I had signed up to join. I looked down at the prayer beads around my wrist that I'd gotten in Lumbini, pulled them off, and shoved them into my pocket. The hardcore spiritual vibe was making me uncomfortable. I thought I had better get over that pretty quickly, considering I had voluntarily come to an ashram in India to study yoga.

As I sat there listening to everyone chew, I began contemplating the nature of the word "spirituality." It didn't make me as uncomfortable as the word "God." But spirituality seemed to connote a relationship with God. The word "God" made me think of organized religion, which, in spite of my Jewish upbringing, made me squirm. On a general level, organized religion felt to me like a cult brainwashing camp, establishing rules of living for people who didn't want to think for themselves. I enjoyed the cultural traditions of Judaism, but was scared of the orthodox. I was scared of Christian fanatics and Islamic jihad. I was scared of Sadhus and the seemingly illogical act of bathing in the ash/debris-infested Ganges. I remembered the way men dunked their babies under that water. Suddenly I felt threatened; I didn't come to the ashram to get brainwashed. I started to panic; what the hell was I doing there?

I took a deep breath, followed by a sip of herbal tea, and reminded myself that I had come because I was desperately seeking an unshakable state of peace and balance within myself. I told myself to be open to what the ashram had to teach me even if it was different or made me uncomfortable; I could then pick and choose what I wanted to apply to my life afterward. I took several bites of my apple before becoming distracted and then disgusted by the silent eating. All the biting, chewing, and swallowing seemed vile. I got up to dump my breakfast in the compost bin and wash my dish. I'd lost my appetite.

I moved from my provisional room to my regular room, shook hands with my three roommates from India, Brazil, and England, then headed down to the main hall for a relaxation session called *yoga nidra*, meaning "yogic sleep." We entered the room, rolled our mats out on the ground, and sat down. Our guide stood at the front of the room and instructed us to lie face up on our mats on the floor and shut our eyes. She proceeded to describe the practice, "The practice of *yoga nidra* is the act of hearing and the act of feeling. In dreams you have no control; in *yoga nidra* you are the creator of the dream." I started squirming inside my skin, uncomfortable again. I told myself to stop both fighting and judging it, and just let it be. I took a deep breath and imagined it reaching all the way to my toes.

"As you lie here this morning, say to yourself, 'I will not sleep. I will practice *yoga nidra*.'" I repeated it to myself and realized I was clenching my jaw hard. I relaxed it and listened as her trance-like voice droned slowly on, "Notice the sounds in the distance. Become aware of the farthest sound. Set an intention. Become aware of your body, scanning from head to toes. Now concentrate on just your right hand. Relax your right thumb, second finger, third finger, fourth finger, fifth finger, palm of the hand, back of the hand, wrist, lower arm, elbow, upper arm..." She continued until she had addressed the whole body and then moved into body/floor awareness, breathing, awareness of sensations, and visualizations. "Imagine that it is very early morning, with just the earliest traces of light, and you are walking alone through a giant field. There is a slight breeze. You see the sun beginning to rise up from behind a mountain in the far distance." I kept falling in and out of consciousness, my mind oscillating between the images she was conjuring and my own dreams. "Bring your awareness back to the dark space in front of your closed eyes... Remember your intention... Become aware of the room... Start moving your body and stretching fingers to toes... The practice of *yoga nidra* is now complete."

I lay in a heap on the ground with my eyes closed, wondering if I would ever be able to move again. My body felt so heavy. I couldn't imagine lifting a limb. Gradually, I began to stretch and roll around on the ground, releasing audible yawns and sighs, until I found myself in child's pose with my hips on my heels, forehead on the mat, arms stretched out in front of me. Gently, I lifted my torso up to sit and eventually to stand. My muscles felt slack, and my mind was so empty that I imagined air blowing in one ear and out the other. I felt like I was moving in slow motion, rolling up my mat and propping it against the wall. I walked outside, observing the process involved in every step. The movement began in the hip, which caused the knee to lift, and then the foot peeled off the ground in a heel-to-toe wave and dropped back down toe to heel on the ground, a couple of feet in front of where it had been before. I continued to observe this until I found a nice spot on the grass to sit down and stare.

Two women, who had also just been in *yoga nidra*, walked by, chatting, and stopped when they saw me. I looked up to see that one was Elisa, my Brazilian roommate. She had sandy-colored hair, blue eyes, and black-rimmed glasses. The sunlight bounced off her lenses into mine, and I squinted. I looked at the other woman, who I had not yet met. She had short curly dark hair, light blue eyes, and was thin with muscular arms.

"Are you all right?" the curly-haired one asked me.

"Oh, yeah, thanks," I said and smiled. I was feeling something unfamiliar and unidentifiable, but since it wasn't anger or anxiousness, it was okay.

They sat down next to me.

"I'm Whitney," curly-hair said, and shook my hand.

The midday sun was beating down hard. Sweat accumulated on my forehead and in my elbow and knee creases. I slowly melted out of my trance.

"Where are you from?" I asked.

"Ottawa, Canada," she said. "You?"

"San Diego, California."

"How did you find out about this place?"

"The Internet, you?"

"Also the Internet!" she exclaimed. "I just scrolled through the website, thought it looked good, and signed up."

I looked over at Elisa, and she nodded in agreement.

I felt a surge of pride at our courage. We had all traveled halfway around the world on our own because we were searching for something deep and fulfilling in our lives and thought this place might help us discover it. Knowing nothing about their backgrounds or what exactly had driven them to make the same decision I had, I felt an immediate, urgent connection. I wiped the sweat off my face. We sat silently, trying to decide what to do with ourselves. We had free time for the rest of the day. It was obscenely quiet.

Elisa finally suggested we leave the ashram for an exploratory walk through the surrounding locale, and Whitney and I obliged. We stood up, wiped the dirt off our pants, and hit the road. We meandered through villages: mud huts with small children wearing just shirts or nothing at all, lined up in a row waving and squealing excitedly, "*Hari Om! Hari Om!*" in their tiny voices. It was the way people greeted each other in this part of India, where in other parts they used "*Namaste*," meaning, "The light within me honors the light within you," a greeting I found beautiful. As our leaders at the ashram greeted us with "*Hari Om*," I came to learn that the phrase literally translates to "The Lord is infinite spirit." To me, the use of the term "Lord" in this case did not have religious implications, which gave the term a bad rap by transforming the idea of the universe's infinite spirit into some ruler in the sky. As an Indian greeting, "Lord" was a label describing that sense of the sublime universe that gives us chills, that mystery. This awareness, with every greeting, heightened my gratitude for being alive.

As we wandered through cow manure–lined roads, past rabid dogs and cows herded by local villagers, we called, "*Hari Om*," to the herders in passing. They wobbled their heads from side to side and grinned. We walked through fields of bright green fresh from monsoon season, past barefoot women in bright saris carrying water, wood, bricks, and cloth on their heads, sweet and humble smiles, holding their daughters' hands.

We chatted through the walk, and I learned that Whitney and Elisa had both just arrived in India the day before; the ashram was their first stop. Elisa was twenty-six, and Whitney was thirty-eight. Elisa had gotten married two years prior and moved to Australia with her husband. Then they had a painful separation, and she decided to come to India to try to figure out the next step in her life. She had a year visa and was planning to travel and find more places to meditate and practice yoga after this program. Whitney was single and worked for child protection services in Ottawa. She had been at the job a year and liked that it was for a meaningful organization, but was still unsatisfied doing full-time administrative work and was looking for something more. There was so much longing as they spoke, their voices rising up from their guts, jutting through their hearts and out their mouths. I shared in their longing. Whitney and Elisa would become my two closest friends.

For such a hard bed, I was able to sleep quite well that night. I passed out around 9:30 p.m. and slept straight through to the wake-up bell at 5:00 a.m., when I woke up sweating and disoriented from my bizarre dream. I dreamt that this man was giving me a massage standing up that turned into a contact dance between the two of us, and then before I knew it, he was raping me through my pants. Then I had an orgasm, went to the bathroom, and peed blood. I would have all kinds of strange dreams at the ashram. Lots of people did. We were told it was part of our detoxification process. Supposedly, all our suppressed fears and emotional disturbances manifested in our dreams so we could see them, release them, and move on.

The first week was the longest of my life. I felt like I was being gassed with tranquilizers, melting in the heat and exhausted by the level of concentration that the whole day required. Space and time were expanding. Everything was slowing down. Every morning, we kicked off our day at 5:45 a.m. with Sanskrit mantra chanting led by a gray-haired Indian woman in a sari. We chanted the thirty names of Durga, followed by Brahma this, Vishnu that. We chanted for increasing mental, physical, and spiritual health, and gave thanks to the sun. Initially, I was wary of the cult-like feel of chanting the names of Hindu gods. The ashram's website had made it very clear that yoga was not a religion, but the science of personal development. Still, why Hindu gods? I eventually came to learn that these were just the chants of the yoga tradition, and it was really more about feeling the physical vibrations of the chanting and the emotional and spiritual impact of a room filled with people generating these vibrations.

Chanting was followed by two hours of yoga postures, called "*asanas*" in Sanskrit. (Sanskrit is the classical language of India, the language in which the original yogic texts and philosophies are recorded.) The yoga was so slow. We didn't even do proper yoga poses the first couple of days, just preparatory movements. "Slowly lift your left arm, bring it down. Circle your hips, even slower. Bend forward at the waist. Come up. Do it again. Lie down on the floor. Lift up your left leg to ninety degrees. Now circle it slowly five times clockwise and five times counterclockwise. The slower, the better." I alternated between feeling the vibe and wanting to shoot myself in the foot.

After morning *asanas*, we had one hour of karma yoga, or service work: cleaning, weeding, or preparing food. Finally at 9 a.m., after four hours of being awake and active, we lined up for our silent breakfast. Then we had one hour of *yoga nidra* and an hour of yoga theory lecture, or two hours of theory lecture. This was followed by lunch, a two-hour break, theory lecture, two more hours of *asanas*, stories and discussions, dinner, and the occasional

evening activity consisting of a yoga documentary or Bhajans: de-
votional Sanskrit songs.

I felt like I'd enrolled in my own temporary prison sentence to
teach me how to live. The parent within me knew this would be
good for me. But on day six out of twenty-four, I was already
counting down the days until I could get out of there. For a place
where we were being taught how to live a more peaceful and happy
existence, my insides felt volatile.

I was in constant dialogue with myself. I felt like I'd been split
in half. One part of me kept saying, Be patient, you are here to
work with your mind that has been so destructive in the past. Yoga
is a vehicle. This is about being in a beautiful remote area with
none of the familiar distractions so you can work on yourself.
Then the other part of me would revolt. Why did you bring me
here? Why is everything so slow? How many days left? It was quite
intense to be studying my mind and how to gain control over it
while simultaneously wrestling with its protests.

I reasoned with myself that this experience was crucial to
both my life and my pursuit of theater and writing. I had to come
at them from a place of grounding within myself because of the
art world's unstable, erratic, and impersonal nature. Even just
thinking about my deep drive to pursue these things caused
squeezing in my chest; the desire was so intense. This month was
going to be hard. I knew it would be, but I couldn't have really
known what that meant until I got there. I felt trapped; all the discipline and concentration the place required left me wanting to
scream much of the time.

The course began on a Wednesday, and Rosh Hashanah, the
Jewish New Year, fell on Saturday night. I had not felt particularly
connected to Judaism in quite some time, but was still moved by
the concepts of Rosh Hashanah: pausing to reflect on my actions
over the past year, assessing how I could be a better person in the
year to come. Before I left San Diego, my mother had photocopies
what she considered the most essential pages from the Rosh Ha-

shanah prayer book for me to read in India. After dinner, I drew the curtains around my bed and sat in lotus position, reading through the pages. The judgment prayer stopped me cold.

On Rosh Hashanah it is inscribed,
And on Yom Kippur it is sealed.
How many shall pass away and how many shall be born,
Who shall live and who shall die...

I had to stop reading to wipe the tears from my eyes. This prayer always so viscerally evoked the memory of being in synagogue with my father after his cancer diagnosis. I remembered it breaking my heart to hear him crying and saying, "I wish my father were here right now. I really miss him." Reading that prayer alone in the middle of rural India, I really missed *my* father. I wondered what he would think about what I'd been doing with my life and wished I could talk to him about it.

It seemed significant that I was engaged in this intensive yoga study over Rosh Hashanah, and at a time when I felt especially in the dark about my future. I tried to convince myself that the future was not important; the present was. And in the present, I was studying the ways of balance and inner peace, committed to doing some serious internal research and working to become the best human I could be. I shut my eyes, rested my palms face up on my knees, and prayed for growth, health, peace, love, and happiness in the coming year. I could do it: I could conquer my anxiety. I could face life with ease. A few more tears slipped down my cheeks.

I was rattled out of my prayer by the sound of the curtain being pulled open. Elisa was standing by my bed.

"Are you coming to Bhajans?" she asked.

Bhajans took place every Saturday night. I didn't feel like going. It seemed wrong to sing Sanskrit yoga songs that mentioned Hindu gods on Rosh Hashanah. But not wanting to isolate myself, I followed her down the stairs and to the main hall. We sat cross-legged against the wall. Volunteers passed out song sheets for us to follow, while two elderly Indian women in saris led us in song from the stage, playing drums and musical shakers. After about ten minutes, everyone around me was singing and dancing up a storm. But I felt too heavy and uncomfortable to join. I slipped out without anyone noticing and went back to my bed to write in my journal, engulfed by a sinking loneliness, really missing my family, especially my mom. Once again, I picked up the Rosh Hashanah packet, reread the judgment prayer about ten times, lay down, and cried myself to sleep.

Every six days, we had one day off to go into the city. I'd been waiting for this first day off since the second day. Finally it arrived, and I slept in until 6:30 a.m., when Whitney, Elisa, and I got up to go for a run while it was still cool out. With my legs pumping, my heart racing, lungs heaving, sweat pouring, for the first time in that week that felt like a year, I was free. Darting through the fields of rural India with Beatles music pumping in my ears was wildly surreal. "*Hari Om!*" squealed the children. "*Hari Om!*" we called back. With the sun and wind in my face, I inhaled the freshness of the fields, and hummed along to "Obladi-Oblada" on my headphones. It was like a dream to be listening to the Beatles while running past cows, mud huts, and women in saris carrying baskets of produce on their heads. We got back to the ashram at about 8:00 a.m., right as the heat was hitting. I showered and eagerly changed into my first non-yoga outfit in a week. I even put on mascara. Taxis would be picking us up after breakfast.

At breakfast, I sat on the ground next to Whitney. We were allowed to talk at meals on our day off. Still, we sat silently, unable to break the habit. In our regular meditative manner, we cut up apples, pears, papayas, and bananas into bite-sized chunks and sprinkled pomegranate seeds over them until our tin bowls housed the same colorful fruit salad we ate every morning. I had filled a bowl with rice and potatoes, but she hadn't taken any. She never ate the rice dish in the morning.

I had tuned into the way Whitney ate from the beginning: She was careful to avoid most starchy carbohydrates, filling her plate with fruits, vegetables, beans, and soup. She ate very slowly, seemingly to savor each bite. By the time she finished cutting up her fruit every morning, most people were already done eating.

After a few bites, I put down my spoon and watched her continue to cut her pear into tiny equal pieces with a sculptor's focus. It took her a little while to notice me noticing her. But once she did, she met my eye, and I quickly looked back at my plate and filled my mouth with two heaping spoonfuls of rice and potato. She continued to carve out her pear.

I took a giant bite of fruit salad and closed my eyes. I chewed slowly as crunchy pear merged with juicy papaya, dissolving into a sweet fruit cocktail on my tongue, the sunlight draping itself across my face. I opened my eyes and looked over at Whitney's hands still hovering over her bowl, cutting her pear. Finally the last chunk dropped. She put down her knife, lifted her spoon, and scooped up a small bit of fruit. Out of the corner of my eye, I watched her raise the spoon to her mouth and take her first bite.

"Not much of a carb eater, huh?" I blurted out.

"No, I guess not," she said.

"Why is that?"

"I'm afraid of getting fat," she said. I was stunned by her bluntness.

I continued to chomp my fruit until I turned to her and without thinking, said, "You know...I had a really serious eating disorder when I was in high school."

"I've had one for most of my life," she said, matter-of-factly, chewing her pear.

I looked her in the eyes, feeling a fierce, desperate connection with her. My pulse quickened, blood rushed to my face. I had felt this kind of intense overwhelming connection with women before several times. It often knocked the wind out of me and left me wondering if I was a lesbian. But I didn't want to have sex with these women, though I often did feel like I was in love with them and thought about kissing them.

"Wow," I said.

"What about you?" she asked. "Do you still struggle with it?"

"You know, I think I'm in denial about it. I know I do, but I don't even acknowledge it to myself. It's certainly not as extreme as it used to be. Still, sometimes I just say fuck it and stuff my face."

"Yeah, I do the same thing, and then I usually throw up."

"Me, too," I said.

I suddenly noticed that everyone else had cleared out of the dining area and gone to the taxis.

"Oh, we gotta go," I said.

"I'm not going to the city."

"Really?"

"Yeah, I want to stay here by myself, relax, go for some walks, you know..."

"Okay," I said, "Well...I should probably get going."

I leaned over and hugged her. She hugged me back, tightly. Our breasts pressed up against the other's, our breaths were colliding. I felt her hand on my back. I wanted to kiss her, but broke away instead.

"Well, have a good day," I said, and ran to meet the taxi. Elisa had saved me a seat next to her.

It was a forty-five-minute rural joyride to the city until we were suddenly absorbed by the chaos of Nasik: no road lanes, honking horns, speeding motorcycles, bright colors, sweet smells, horrific smells, crowds. We had only been at the ashram one week, but the days felt so long and removed from city life that I experienced a renewed culture shock when I exited the taxi. My mind was also completely blown by the fact that I had arrived only one week before; it felt like it had been months.

We had until 5:00 p.m. to run wild. Elisa and I both eyed the coffee shop next to the office, then looked back at each other and made a mad dash for the door. After adhering to the strict ashram diet, we suddenly turned into caffeine- and sugar-crazed monsters, shamelessly devouring chocolate blended coffee drinks and two warm brownies with ice cream and hot fudge, then running our fingers across the remaining fudge on the plates and sucking the life out of them. Leaning back in our seats, we slipped inside the blaring Indian music and into a sugar-induced coma. I thought about what my nutritionist said when I was recovering from anorexia: Depriving oneself will always lead to binging. Then I thought about Whitney. The way she was able to maintain so much control over the way she ate made me jealous. Part of me wanted to challenge myself to be like that again, knowing that was certainly a backward step from the path toward balance. The ashram depriving us completely of all familiar comfort food was not actually that balancing, though. Come to think of it, practicing four hours of *asanas* and attending three hours of yoga theory lectures was not exactly balanced, either.

I rubbed my full belly guiltily, feeling pangs of confusion shoot through my chest. Was the ashram really going to help me? Part of me felt straitjacketed there, making me desperately want to run from it. Again, a bigger part kept saying that it was good for me, even necessary, but man, it was hard to be there. And even though I was sitting with Elisa in the coffee shop, I felt painfully alone. I had only known her a week; we were still practically strangers. I missed talking to my mom and my sister. Shifting my weight in my seat, my chest filled up with longing and my eyes brimmed with tears.

"Man, that was awesome," said Elisa in her cute Brazilian accent, sitting up and slurping up the remaining glob of liquid from her glass.

"Yeah..." I muttered, my eyes lingering on the surface of the table.

"Are you okay?

I squirmed in my seat and clenched my fists.

"I don't know. I feel uncomfortable. I really do know that there's a lot to be gained from this whole experience, but at the same time, I'm counting down the days until it's over. Not that I really have somewhere to go or something specific to do after this. I just feel so worked up all the time. But that's why I'm here, you know, to try to stop this. I don't know... I just... Ahhhh...."

I squirmed more, squeezed my fists, and dug my nails into my thighs. Elisa scooted her chair toward me and put her hand on my shoulder.

"It's okay," she said, and I sat for a moment, breathing into her hand, always grateful for even the smallest dose of physical affection.

"You're right—there is a lot to be gained here," she said, squeezing my shoulder. "You just have to relax and let yourself gain it."

"I know...thank you," I said, leaning my head against her shoulder.

She ran her fingers through my hair. My head rose and fell against her as she breathed. I closed my eyes while the sound of dueling sitars superimposed my thoughts.

We spent the rest of the afternoon walking around historical Old Nasik. We wandered in the heat through crowds of people and cows, visiting ancient temples and colorful marketplaces, where we entertained the broken English of smiling vendors, examining handmade crafts, jewelry, and incense. We continued on until we found ourselves strolling beneath a canopy of trees along a river on the edge of town, where eventually we found a nice quiet place to sit and stare at the water. The still river sparkled in the sunlight. We sat for a few minutes in silence, our breaths synchronizing with the rhythm of the soft breeze.

"Everything that's happening right now feels completely unreal," I said, turning toward her. "I feel like I must be dreaming."

"I know what you mean."

"There's no way we're going to be the same once this is over. I wonder how it'll feel to be back home."

"Yeah, I can't imagine it. But I guess there's really no point in thinking about that right now."

"Yeah, you're right." I uncrossed and re-crossed my legs, arched my back, and felt the sun on my face.

As we resumed staring at the water, the pangs in my chest morphed from pained confusion to fierce gratitude. I had wanted to come here and do this, and I'd made it happen. Maybe I wouldn't go back to the States when this was over. Maybe I would extend my visa for a year, volunteer, work on farms, travel, and teach. I really could do anything I wanted; I just had to decide what that was. I looked over at Elisa. Swimming in her own thoughts, she didn't notice me looking at her. I gazed back ahead. The blue of the sky was fading with the sinking sun. I looked down at my watch to see that time had completely warped; soon the taxis would be meeting us at the office.

"We have to go," I said, tapping Elisa on the shoulder, waking her from her daze.

"Oh, okay, yeah," she said, shaking her head.

We stood up slowly and drifted back to the office through the crowded, chaotic city streets where the rickshaws, motorcycles, and cars flew, swerved, and honked amidst swirling colors and smells. Without conscious awareness, as if something had lifted us up and carried us there, we reached the office and boarded the taxis with the rest of our group. On the ride back, we did not speak, and the surrounding chatter progressively dissolved into an unintelligible buzzing. Out the window, the pink sky cast a neon glow on the green grass. Men walked along the road in ragged clothing leading cows, smiling at us through worn faces as we passed. As we pulled up to the gate of the ashram, my chest felt very heavy and sore, my eyes once again brimming with tears. I felt insanely grateful to be alive. That night, I went to bed promising myself that from then on, all my actions would be done mindfully and with love. I felt a deep pull toward healing work and decided this was my calling. Sleep brought with it a sense of peace and resolution.

Ninety to One Hundred Years

The next morning, I woke under my mosquito netting feeling like an elephant was sitting on my chest. I felt trapped and wanted to run. Why had my sense of well-being flown the coop? At mantra chanting, my mouth was moving and the sounds were coming out, but I was sweating madly and my thoughts were racing. *"Om trayambakam yajamahe..." Get me out of here. I want to leave, but I don't know where to go. "...sugandhim pushtivardhanam..." What am I doing? "...urvarukamiva bandhanat..." What is life for? "...mrityromukshiya mamritat." Why do I feel trapped in my skin?* The meaning of the complete Sanskrit phrase was, "I offer my regards to Lord Shiva, please give me best of health (physical, mental and spiritual). Free me from all bondages and give me immortality by saving me from untimely death." We chanted it eleven times, as I continued battling my thoughts and mounting anxiety.

The feelings only escalated during morning *asanas*. I flung myself from pose to pose, feeling increasingly angry and irritable, straining in the poses, making my muscles hurt, savoring the pain. I scrawled frantic, confused streams of consciousness in my notebook during anatomy lecture and didn't speak to anyone unless spoken to, and then my responses were always short and clipped. After lunch, I took a nap for a break from this unbearable state.

At the end of *asana* class before dinner, I had to lie down during fast breathing exercises. It made me far too dizzy to participate. Lying on my mat while the rest of the class breathed heavily and audibly, I envisioned a man slamming into me, fucking me harder and harder with each fast breath. God, I wished he would just tear me apart. At the class's closing, I sat up and chanted eleven *oms* while visualizing a hand tearing through my sternum and squeezing my heart. I was struck by a sudden craving for experimental theater work, deeply needing to physically and vocally release all this emotion and energy. Yoga is so much about control, but I was feeling out of control; I wanted to get up onstage into a character in a high-stakes situation so I could flail, cry, and scream. I was craving performing so much I could feel it literally ripping through my chest, clawing at my heart, shouting, *Come on, hop to it, you lazy bitch.* Sweating and burning up, there was so much energy inside me, so much yearning. What was one to do with all this energy on an ashram surrounded by poisonous snakes? Where was one to go?

At dinner, as I sat on the floor eating my lentil soup and boiled vegetables, I felt myself burning internally. I knew Whitney was watching me all through dinner. I was watching her, too. We slyly observed how the other filled her plate, how fast she ate, what was left over. She sat on the ground across from me, and while we were both completely aware of the other, no eye contact was made. Instead, we ate our meals in our customary silence. And when we were done eating, we each got up onto our knees, sat back on our heels, closed our eyes, and prayed.

Directing my closed eyes toward the space between my eyebrows, I prayed to contain all this energy. Feeling a million fireworks shooting from all directions exploding in my chest, I lightly rocked my torso back and forth. I stayed with all the sensations, heart open, spine erect. I felt the fist release my heart and sink past my sternum into my stomach. I felt it clenching and releasing, creating violent waves of stomach acid. Lower even, plunging through intestines, uterus, cervix, into my vaginal canal: clenching, pounding, clenching, pounding. My whole body shook.

After dinner, Kate, the ashram leader, announced there would be an activity in the main hall. We filed in to find Gandhar, the son of the ashram's founder, sitting onstage in full lotus position with a small brown box in his lap. He was a tall, thin Indian man with dark brown eyes that popped and was insanely limber, likely the result of practicing yoga from an early age. A soft white light shone on his face; the rest of the room was dim.

"Tonight we will be having a question-and-answer session," he announced slowly and deliberately, extending his boney arms out to the sides, his long fingers curling toward the ceiling. "Everyone who would like may take a second to anonymously write a question relating to yoga on a piece of paper and put it in this box, and I will answer it to the best of my ability."

He stood up and walked the box down to a girl sitting at the foot of the stage, then returned to his center-stage lotus position. Some people took out notebooks and pens and wrote questions; I just passed the box along. In the moment, I couldn't organize my thoughts to formulate an intelligent question. Aside from the sound of writing and the box being passed from hand to hand, the room was silent and still. Eventually, the box found its way back to Gandhar.

"Before we address these questions, I would like us all to do a meditation exercise together." He smiled. "Now, trying to get the mind to focus and meditate is like asking a drunken monkey bit by scorpions to be still."

We all laughed.

"That's why simple exercises like the one we're about to do can help ease you into it," he said. "Please sit with your eyes closed; head up; chin tucked; shoulders, chest, and face relaxed. Begin to tune into your breath, not doing anything to strain it or change it. Just notice it entering and exiting the body without effort, as it always does, twenty-four hours a day. This is your life force. Take a deep inhale and extend your arms out to the sides. Then bring your hands forward, palms cupped toward your belly button, hovering above your lap. Keep your elbows bent out to the sides. As you inhale, allow your hands to ascend slowly, passing your belly button, ribs, sternum, chest, throat, face, and lift up over your head, palms still facing you. Then, on your exhale, just as slowly, allow your hands to float back down, passing your face, throat, chest, sternum, ribs, belly, and, once again, let them hover lightly above your lap. Then repeat the process twice more... Now, bring your palms toward each other so they are very close but not quite touching. What do you feel?"

"Energy," emitted a woman's voice that rose up from her core, solid and strong.

"Magnetism," someone else said.

"Charge."

I agreed with all three; there was definitely an energetic magnetic charge between my palms. I also had the relieving sensation of empty darkness behind my eyes. My breathing felt easy, chest and shoulders melting.

"Good," said Gandhar. "Release your hands to your sides and gently let your eyes float open, allowing the light to slowly creep in, keeping the gaze soft. I will now answer your questions."

He reached into the box and pulled out a slip of paper. First, he read it silently to himself.

"Will yoga help me overcome fear?" he read aloud, then looked up. "Well, yes," he said. "Practicing yoga puts you in touch with the realities of life. When you realize that you have ninety to one hundred years in your life, if you're lucky, and then you will be gone, when you really absorb that truth with the whole of your being, all sense of fear related to life experiences just falls away."

When he said that, I felt shivers up my spine, and my fingers went numb. Of course, I was already aware that death loomed at the end of the road, but I had never really allowed it to sink in. How could I? But in that moment, in that dimly lit silent room in front of the skinny Indian man with the soft white light on his face, my insides shook as this revelation infused every part of me. My palms were clammy, my heart was thumping madly against my rib cage, my jaw locked. I felt the blood drain from my face as I sat there, frozen in terror. I really would die one day.

That night, I had a dream that I was sitting in the living room of my old house late at night with my father. In the dream, I had woken up to go to the kitchen for some water and saw him sitting on the couch. The lamp on the end table was on, the one with the old dusty shade. My dad looked like he was deeply lost in thought. I sat down next to him.

He turned his head toward me, smiled, and patted the back of my right hand.

"You're a good kid," he said. "You know that, right?"

Kid. I was my current age in the dream: twenty-six. Of course, I'd always be his kid.

I smiled back at him. He turned his head away slowly, still lost in thought. The lamplight poured over his blue and gray checkered pajama bottoms.

All I could hear were crickets. We'd had a cricket infestation in our house for years. They came out at night and littered the carpet, must have been getting in through some crack in some screen somewhere. We never determined quite how to get rid of them, so they just became part of the family. I was listening to the crickets as I sat on the couch next to my ruminating dad when my cat brushed up against my leg. Just a soft brush of fur, and I was so startled I nearly had a heart attack.

The yellow light from the lamp turned orange, then red.

"Dad?"

"Yeah?"

"I went alone to this ashram in India. I just had an intuitive sense it was something I needed to do."

"Okay," he said, shifting his weight. His dark eyes and salt and pepper hair shone under the red light. The cat jumped up onto his lap and startled me again. My dad didn't flinch, but stroked her fur methodically with his gaze forward and steady.

"Yeah, so I went there to study yoga, you know, learn some ancient wisdom about balance. I thought it would be good for me, help me deal with the uncertainty of life."

He nodded, gaze still forward, and the cat jumped off his lap.

"Well, one night, we were having this discussion about fear."

The lamplight turned blue. We both remained unfazed by the changing colors.

"Someone asked the teacher, 'Will yoga help me get over my fear?' and the teacher said, 'Yes. Yoga will. Yoga brings you more in touch with the truth that your time on earth is finite.' Well, when he explained that, it really shook me. I got chills and goose bumps everywhere."

My dad, soaked in blue, just nodded.

"You're a good kid," he said, and patted my right hand. "Do you want something to drink? How about a chocolate egg cream? I'll make it right now."

But he didn't move. Instead, the skin on his chin started to sag. His face looked like it was beginning to melt.

"Dad, are you okay?"

"Yeah, why?"

His lower eyelids and earlobes were leaking down his face. His hair was falling off his head in clumps onto his shoulders.

"Maybe I should make it," I suggested, and started to get up. "Maybe you should just relax."

"I can make it," he said. "No problem."

The cat jumped onto my lap, and I screamed. She scratched my cheek. I closed my eyes and brought my palm to my face. When I opened my eyes, the lamplight was purple, and my dad's face had almost completely disappeared. Just his mouth, his long ears, and the clumps of hair on his shoulders remained.

"You're a good kid," said the mouth.

As the light turned black, the crickets seemed to get louder.

Ninety to a hundred years if you're lucky, I thought as I got up to make myself a chocolate egg cream.

My dad seemed so real in the dream. But when I woke up in the morning, I remembered that he was dead. I didn't feel sad, though. I didn't feel anything. I just remembered.

The morning rolled in with an unprecedented sense of calm. I chanted mantras with a clear mind, allowing the vibrations from my throat to merge with those of the rest of the room and fill me up, head to toe. In *asana* class, I flowed from pose to pose with grace and ease, my breath in line with my movements, mind relaxed, and when class was over, I could not believe two hours had passed. The rest of the day was like floating down a river on a raft under a warm sun. I was cracking jokes for the first time since I had been there, smiling and laughing, feeling like I was finally merging with the community. Tranquility stretched out its limbs and breathed with ease inside my chest.

Over the next few days, I felt myself settling into the ashram's pace and routine and was getting really drawn into the yoga theory lectures. One morning, we had a whole lecture about the meaning and chanting of *Om*. Pournima Mandlik, the wife of the ashram's creator and owner, gave us this lecture. She was a woman of about seventy who possessed an inner vitality like nothing I had ever seen. Her mere presence elevated the energy in the room, her unshakable smile exuding contagious passion. We sat in our chairs with notebooks open, pens in hand, hungry for her wisdom.

She stood radiantly at the front of the room in a sari swirling with purples and pinks, gray hair pulled back, the light from the window bouncing off her exuberant cheeks.

"Today we are going to talk about chanting *Om*," she began in her high-pitched Indian accent, gesturing wildly with her arms, face all lit up. "*Om* chanting is the shortest and most powerful yoga practice. *Om* represents energy. Energy has four qualities: light, heat, vibrations, and sound. The whole universe is vibrating with *Om*. When we chant that sound, we join with universal energy. Chanting just one *Om* will make a human being calm and quiet, increasing concentration, confidence, and energy."

She grew more excited with every word, her voice increasing in volume and pitch, her arms extended out to her sides, eyes widening. "Chanting *Om* creates *prana*, the energy we take in. *Prana* is composed of the two Sanskrit words *Pra* and *Nav*, meaning 'force-fully new.' Chanting *Om* allows you to create new things with your body, mind, spirit, intelligence, and emotions! If you keep chanting *Om*, laziness will vanish from your life. You will overcome all obstacles. You will be unstoppable!"

She was practically jumping up and down. The light from the window was bright on her face. Her smile was huge, her chest open, face soft, feet light on the ground. She was nearly floating in space. We were all jotting down notes furiously, determined to channel the power of *Om* in the way she was describing. That's why we had all journeyed to the ashram in the first place, because we craved the catharsis of exploding through our mind-made suffering into our lives with boundless positive energy. After that lecture, I spent several days without so much as one knot of anxiety; my chest felt free and light. I smiled without needing a reason, breathed deeply without effort, and was not caught in the loop of replaying the past or fretting about the future. I relished my rebirth as a positive, balanced human being, really wanting to believe that it would last.

Vomen

After chanting, Kate led us through a one-hour *asana* session, then informed us that we would be practicing the cleansing technique, *vomen*.

"*Vomen* is a technique for cleansing the stomach. This practice has many benefits; it is especially good for people with high acidity, indigestion, and anxiety. We will head down to the road in front of the ashram and drink six glasses of warm salt water, then immediately vomit it up. It is to be done on an empty stomach, as the objective is not to throw up food, but to clean the walls of the stomach. The salt in the water will prevent the stomach acid from burning the throat."

I could hardly believe what I was hearing. We were actually going to make ourselves vomit as part of a class. In my head, I began formulating the letter to my mother: *Dear Mom, Today in class, our teacher made us drink warm salt water until we vomited. Also, our lecture yesterday was about merging with the infinite. How's the cat? Love you.* My mind flashed back to the many times my head had hung over the toilet bowl while I violently hurled up the partially digested remnants of a binge. It had been about a year since the last time I had done it.

Kate continued, "Often the water comes right back up without effort. If not, you can stick a finger down your throat to bring it up. Be sure your fingernails are short so as not to cut the back of your throat. I have nail clippers up here if you need them. Once you have completed the practice, please return to the hall and lie down in *shavasana* for at least ten minutes to fully absorb the ef-

fects." She paused. "Now, if you have reservations about partici-
pating for psychological reasons, you may abstain. But I really do
encourage you to participate. Just think, when else are you going to
have experienced people around to support and supervise you?"

I almost laughed out loud. Who in that room was actually
planning to do this back home?

"Please follow me. Jane will demonstrate." Jane was one of
the volunteers. Still sitting on our yoga mats, we looked around the
room and eyed each other apprehensively, then slowly stood up
and followed Kate out the door and down to the road. Jane stood
beside two big silver bowls of warm salt water and glasses, smiled,
and waved to us as we approached. I looked beyond her at the
expansive green rice field, then up at the distant mountains and
finally at the sky, clear and blue as ever.

"Hi, everyone," she said. "So, there's really not that much to
this. The important thing is to drink all six glasses as quickly as
possible. Usually when I do that, I lean over and it comes right out.
I always feel really good after; you will, too."

We watched her chug six cups of water in rapid succession.
Then, as she leaned over, the liquid streamed out of her nose and
mouth like a waterfall onto the green grass, glittering in the
sunlight. When she had emptied herself, she stood up, wiped her
mouth, smiled, and said, "Okay, your turn."

Elisa burst into tears.

"I'm sorry, I can't do this," she sobbed.

Whitney went to hug her. Elisa cried on her shoulder a few
moments, then pressed herself away and crossed her arms over her
chest.

"It's okay," said Kate. "You don't have to. You can have a seat
and relax, or, if you'd feel more comfortable, you can go rest in
your room."

"I think I want to go to my room," she said.

"Okay," said Kate. "We'll be here if you need anything."

Elisa turned and headed back up the hill.

"Is everyone else okay?" Kate asked.

We nodded. I was still nervous.

Jane passed out cups to all of us. We lined up behind the bowls, and I watched the people in front of me begin to chug one cup after another. Just watching made me gag. Finally, I was up. Jane ladled me a cup full of warm salt water. I looked into the cup and told myself not to think. I brought the cup to my lips, tilted my head back, and dumped the liquid down my throat. I already felt like retching, but before I knew it my cup had been filled once again, and I was bringing it back up to my lips and repeating the process. After the fourth, my stomach was protesting angrily, but I still had to force two more down. Once the final cup was emptied, I felt like I would burst.

I leaned over, and the water exploded out of me. Some shot through my nose, and the salt burned. The water continued to gush out in sheets, my mind emptying with my stomach. The grass below was a spiraling green blur. I shoved my fingertips into my guts, forcing more water up and out. I shoved my fingertips back in; more flew out. I was becoming addicted to the sensation of deep purging. *Get it out of me. Please get it out of me, all of it, everything that's bad and negative. I want to be clean and fresh, I want to be free.* I continued to press my fingers into my guts until nothing was left. But I didn't feel done. I stuck my index and middle finger down the back of my throat: still nothing. It was over. I coughed my way up to standing and caught sight of the rest of the people lined up along the road on either side of me, completing their *vomen* practice.

Wiping my mouth with the back of my hand, I headed up the hill to the main hall, where my yoga mat awaited. I lay down on my back, closed my eyes, and placed one hand on my chest and one hand on my belly, feeling my heart thump through my whole body and my lungs heave. Tunneling my gaze into the back of my closed lids, black morphed into red, which morphed to gold. Suddenly, out of nowhere, I was flooded with a barrage of childhood memories. I rarely thought about childhood and often had difficulty remembering much that happened before middle school, so I was stunned by the clarity and vividness of the memories that rushed through me.

I remembered being chased around the playground by boys in preschool, then coming back to the classroom for animal crackers and apple juice before napping on cots. I remembered the smell of paste in kindergarten, sitting on the floor for story time, learning the Pledge of Allegiance, learning the alphabet and writing words, then sentences, and loving to write my name everywhere. First grade brought with it a greater love of writing; I began folding stacks of paper in half, stapling the edges and writing short stories as well as lengthy journal entries reflecting on my day, my friends, what I liked and disliked about what was happening around me. I remembered being in second grade about to take a test when Mr. Green said no one could raise their hands or get out of their chairs until everyone finished. In the middle of the test, I had to pee very badly, but I knew I was not allowed to get up, so I thought if I just let a little bit out, it would be okay. A little bit of course led to emptying my whole bladder, and the result was a big puddle on the floor. I remembered the sting of shame and embarrassment when my friend grabbed paper towels from the back of the room and helped me clean it up. I remembered being in third grade and making an elaborate castle out of a cardboard box, being in fourth grade writing about the kelp forest, being in fifth grade in leggings and oversized T-shirts, doing a report on Helen Keller and dressing as her for Open House. That was the last image that flashed before again all I saw was gold, then red, then black.

My focus returned to my breath and heartbeat, which had normalized. I let my arms fall to my sides, then reached them overhead and stretched my body in opposing directions. I rolled onto my right side and pressed myself up to sitting in a cross-legged position, my spine straight. Then I began to watch my thoughts, blowing across my mind like wind. I felt nostalgic for childhood; I missed being cared for as I had been then. I was wrestling with the reality of being an adult and all the stress I'd been having about finding my footing. My mind flashed to the crowded New York City streets where I would soon be returning, where bills and student loan payments awaited, where I had no job. Sudden panic. I breathed in deeply, held the air in as long as I could, then exhaled that thought. *No tension, no anxiety. Not here, not now.* Amazed at how I was able to let the thought slip away, I decided *vomen* technique really was good for anxiety. Slowly coming to standing, I got up to find that my karma yoga assignment for the day was cleaning the main hall. I had never mopped a floor with such presence and grace.

Silence

After dinner, Kate told us that the next day would be spent in complete silence. We would chant in the morning and could ask questions in lectures, but otherwise we were to remain quiet. No social chatter. "It's a practice to encourage mindfulness," she explained.

It was raining when I hopped out of bed at 5 a.m. the next morning, the first ashram rain. As my roommates and I walked to the meditation hall, the sky looked like a smeared watercolor painting, drippy streaks of orange and pink against the gray. I'd never realized how loud our clomping feet sounded against the dirt road. We chanted and practiced *asanas* as usual. Then Kate announced karma yoga assignments. I would be in the kitchen that morning, helping to prepare breakfast. I emerged from the hall to see the sun had risen as usual, but it was muffled by gray. The gray only intensified the feeling of rumination elicited by group silence.

I made my way through the drizzle to the kitchen, where I sat down cross-legged on the concrete floor beside the three other women on kitchen duty and the three main Indian kitchen ladies, who wordlessly instructed us on how to proceed. We were handed chopping blocks, knives, and cucumbers, carrots and potatoes to be peeled and chopped, as well as apples and pears to be washed and placed in bowls. As I chopped carrots beneath this dome of silence, I became acutely aware of every sound, which together created a unique orchestral arrangement: the steady rhythm of knives against chopping blocks, the scraping of peelers against potatoes and cucumbers, the perpetual plopping of fruit into bowls of water, bare feet pattering on the ground each time someone got up to grab something from the other side of the kitchen, the light tapping of the rain against the thin roof, and the undercurrent of everyone's varied breathing patterns. I lost myself in the sounds as I worked, and the hour was up before I knew it. In the midst of my daze, I set the bowls of fruit on each table. Then someone rang the breakfast bell, and everyone lined up to eat.

As I spooned my spiced potato, carrot, and cucumber stew and listened to the sounds of chewing and tin cups clanking against tabletops, I thought about silence. I thought about the greater part of a year and a half I'd spent squirming inside my skin, barely able to speak because I was so consumed by the absurd concept of language that my brain had obliterated the meaning of words and detached my voice from my self. I closed my eyes and sighed with relief that I was eventually able to overcome this.

I thought about how the air was constantly congested with the sounds of tangled voices in daily life and how comforting it was to be in the company of others but have a break from all the droning chatter. After finishing breakfast, there was still twenty minutes before our lecture, so I sat out on the damp concrete in front of the dining area and stared at the foggy mountains. Moments later, I heard footsteps sneaking up behind me and turned to see Elisa. We smiled at each other and she sat down next to me, her shoulder touching mine. We sat for a few minutes together, staring at the mountains, then I rested my head against her shoulder and she put her arm around me. I realized then how often I used talking as a shield, a way to fill space between others and myself. Actually being in silence with another person dissolved that shield, making me feel much more vulnerable. Sitting with Elisa, the more I breathed, the more relieved I felt. No pressure to say or do anything, just two people, sitting together, being. Soon the rain picked back up, so we stood and headed to the main hall for the morning lecture on Kundalini yoga.

On my slow walk up the hill in the rain, I continued to reflect on silence. I thought about how often people spoke without thinking and how once something was said, it could never be taken back. I thought about how various things people had said to me were stitched into the fabric of my consciousness, like "I love you" or "you're beautiful" or "that was terrible" or "you're wrong." Words are powerful. This silence practice was definitely about becoming more mindful of what we said out loud, considering what its effects might be.

Space and time expanded in the silence. Our two-hour break after lunch enveloped me in its cocoon. My roommates and I lay on our beds. I stared out my window, watching the rain melt my view of the rippling grass, dissolving inside the rhythm of tapping raindrops against our roof. As the day progressed, I plunged deeper into myself inside this well of silence. As I moved through space, I was aware of the environment and the people around me, but with each passing hour, consciousness felt more like lucid dreaming, the gray grew grayer, green grew greener, air grew thicker, the sky seemed to be sinking.

In *asana* class, as I moved from pose to pose, I felt like a puppet being manipulated by the voice of our guide; my movements seemed to be happening effortlessly. My body felt feather-like, muscles, bones, and organs disintegrating with each swan dive, side bend, half lift. Melting into corpse pose at the end of class, my gaze drilled into the back of my lids, and blackness swallowed me up as my mind and body disappeared. I wanted to remain in this motionless state for a long time, free of struggle, desire, interaction, relieved by the nothingness of peace. Suddenly, thoughts rapid fired through me like laser beams: *My conception of reality is entirely based on my upbringing and the stories I tell myself. This is blazingly apparent in the absence of money exchange, jobs, city life, family, friends, and everything else familiar. I used to think that enlightenment was just an ideal to strive for, a myth to motivate, not something that could actually be achieved, but I now believe it is possible. There is a way to live without being a blind slave to my cravings. I can be patient and kind to others and myself. No more fits of anxiety, no more deep dark depression, no more trashing myself, de-*

stroying myself, hating myself, calm mind, open heart, able to handle anything that comes my way. I will find a romantic partner. I will achieve creative success. I will train myself not to take things personally, become peaceful, blissful, fully realized. My core pulsed with the enormity of these desires.

Suddenly a soft external voice cascaded over the one exploding in my head. "Slowly bring your attention back to the body."

I couldn't feel my body; maybe it had become part of the floor.

"Begin to deepen the breath. Wiggle your fingers and toes."

My fingers and toes would not comply. I had never felt so heavy.

"Let your head roll from side to side."

After two inhalations and exhalations, I was able to manage this, but they were the slowest movements I had ever made. I could have walked across two New York City blocks in the time it took for me to move my head from side to side.

"Keeping your eyes closed, roll onto your side in your own time and gently press yourself up to sitting in a comfortable cross-legged position. Let your palms rest face up on your knees. Let your spine be straight. Reconnect with the intention you set at the beginning of class."

Eleven *oms* later, my torso was folded forward over my crossed legs and my forehead was on the ground, arms stretched out overhead, palms together.

"Surrender yourself to your God, your Guru, Mother Nature, Supreme Consciousness, the energy within you. *Hari Om.*"

I surrender. Now please let me stay here forever.

The room cleared, leaving me alone in that position for the forty-five minutes of free time before dinner. When I finally slow-motion dragged myself back up to sitting, my breathing was shallow and my arms hung out of my shoulder sockets like limp noodles. I floated into the wet night like a shadow, surrounded by a flurry of nameless faceless bodies, lucid dreaming inside a giant mushroom cloud.

Teaching

The next morning, in our first lecture of the day, Kate talked to us about the practical elements of becoming a yoga teacher. Up until that point, we had been chanting, practicing *asanas*, and studying yoga history and theory, but it was now time to apply it all to actually teaching students of our own. That afternoon, we would begin micro lessons. Our twenty-person group would be split into three, and, in these smaller groups, we would practice teaching small parts of a class, working our way up to teaching for a full hour. A volunteer would sit with each group to give people individual feedback. I had to wonder, could I really guide other people toward inner balance and peace when I felt so volatile and unsettled? I would be teaching the exact thing I needed to learn most, but maybe this was the best way to really learn it.

It would seem that teaching yoga would be the perfect way to marry my theater and massage therapy training. However, I actually felt nervous about standing in front of the group and instructing them. As an actor, I had experience playing roles in a fictitious heightened reality. As a massage therapist, the client's awareness of me as a person dissolved inside my touch. But as a yoga teacher, I would have to stand as my transparent self, nothing between me and the group looking to me for relief from the stresses of their lives. When I walked to the front of the room to teach my first micro lesson, time slowed and my heart raced. As I turned to face the group, my cheeks were on fire, and I couldn't feel my feet. All I had to teach was one preparatory movement, a physical warm-up leading into *asana* practice. I shook out my hands, took a breath, exhaled hard and audibly through my mouth, and looked down at the ground. When I looked back up, everyone was sitting cross-legged on their mats, smiling at me, completely unthreatening. I realized I was loading all the pressure on myself, as usual. I smiled back, but my heart was still racing.

"Hello, everyone, today we are going to practice Preparatory Movement Number Four," I announced, tentatively. "Please stand at the front of your mat, legs straight, toes and heels together, chest open, shoulders relaxed, and bring your hands to prayer position, thumbs touching your sternum. Take a second to close your eyes and inhale deeply into your thumbs." As I spoke, my heart rate gradually slowed, and I came to feel a strong pulse through the tips of my fingers. "Now gently open your eyes and bring your hands to your waist. Inhale lifting the chest to the ceiling, exhale, and bend forward with a flat back, bringing your nose toward your knees." My voice was becoming more sure of itself. Instructing the movements was becoming its own meditation. My focus was transferring from myself to the six people in front of me moving along the current of my words. "Maintaining a flat back, slowly inhale yourself back up to standing. Once again, bring your hands back to heart center, thumbs touching your sternum. Close your eyes and inhale deeply into your thumbs." I followed my own instructions, my thumbs digging into my sternum, breath ballooning out of my lungs, varied shades of black and red swirling behind my closed lids. I exhaled fully as my lungs deflated, opened my eyes, and allowed my gaze to float steadily from face to face. "*Namaste*," I said.

"*Namaste*," they all said in unison, opening their eyes slowly and smiling once again. My heart was vibrating against my ribs, and a sudden feeling of love toward the people in the room surged through my chest so forcefully, I nearly fell over. I returned to a seated position on my mat and waited eagerly for feedback from the volunteer.

"You have a very warm, clear voice," she said. "You spoke at a nice pace and seemed very present. You're going to be an excellent teacher."

"Thank you," I said, smiling as a warm sensation spread through my body. As the next person stood up to instruct, I realized I really did want to teach yoga and was giddily looking forward to resuming micro lessons after the upcoming day off.

So Fucking Peaceful

Elisa and I went for a buffet Indian lunch in the city, and I ate something that burned a hole through my stomach. Whether it was the spicy eggplant, vegetable masala, or cauliflower kari that did it, I had severe diarrhea for several days and could barely lift my head off my pillow, let alone get up at 5 a.m. to chant and practice yoga or teach a micro lesson. I was writhing and flopping around in my bed by myself, crying and sweltering in the heat. There was no television to watch, no phone, and everyone else was busy with the daily schedules. All the beautiful revelations seemed to have fallen away as it was just me, alone in my room on the hard mattress, wrestling with the old thoughts once again.

How am I going to support myself when I get back to New York? Life really is a solitary journey; how do I transcend this aching loneliness? How do I work with my thoughts so they don't cause me so much suffering? Is inner peace really possible? Is love really possible? I wish I could take a pill to knock me out. My stomach really hurts. I wish I could practice yoga with everyone. I'm ready to break my goddamn arm... Okay, I will calm myself down: This is exactly what I am training to do here. Back to the breath. This will pass. Everything passes. I am calm. I am peaceful. So fucking peaceful. Goddamn it. Fuck you, body. Fuck you, brain.

For the first couple of days of my illness, I had legitimately lost my appetite, and my stomach immediately ejected anything I tried to eat. Then, as my stomach finally started to relax, I decided I still didn't feel like eating much. It had been about ten years since I'd experimented with starvation, and after a few days of hardly any food, I decided to see how long I could go while eating as little as possible. At first, it was my way of backlashing against my own body for putting me through such hell. Then, after several meals of eating three to four bites of soup or rice, I began to think about the yogis who renounce everything, including food and water, sit on a mountain top stripped of their egos, waiting to merge with supreme consciousness. I decided this near-fasting would be for spiritual purposes, a way of training myself to be content with less. The ashram was about distilling our needs to their most basic. Maybe I could starve myself into self-realization. If I didn't need food, I could just climb the hill behind the ashram and sit with my eyes closed in lotus position until enlightenment exploded like lightning out of every orifice. Then I would run naked through the fields, smearing mud all over my body, shrieking madly, leaping and spinning—free at last.

Sitting at meals, I wondered where the others were looking while they ate their food in silence. I looked out into the distance, not at any point in particular, just out. The deafening silence underlying the vile chewing made me acutely aware of the fact that everyone was eating. I found myself paying greater attention to the few bites I chose to consume, studying every spoonful: the colors, quantity, and texture, and smelling everything before parting my lips and dropping the food onto my tongue. I thought about the process of digestion: how the food was just on the tongue for a mere fifteen to twenty seconds before sliding down the esophagus, into the stomach, breaking down and circulating through the body for eighteen hours, nourishing every system, every cell before waste was expelled. Nourishment—right. This was the function of food. But the body adapts. The less one consumes, the less one needs to consume. Of course, if there is nothing to digest, the body begins to digest itself. We are what we eat. If we eat nothing, then we are nothing. I was curious about what being nothing would feel like.

One day at lunch, I served myself a few spoonfuls of lentil soup, beet salad, and brown rice. After some deliberation, I grabbed a piece of *chapatti* (Indian flat bread), but knew immediately I would not allow it into my body. I sat down and examined my beautiful spoonfuls of beet salad and brown rice in perfect proportion: one-third rice and two-thirds beets. The beets were a radiant purple cut into six perfect pieces, and the rice was sticky. After staring at the plate, I began to eat, but very slowly, maintaining long pauses after swallowing each bite. I ripped a small bit off my *chapatti*, then put it down. Eventually, the girl next to me pointed to it, silently asking for it. I obliged, sat with my back against the wall, closed my eyes, and listened to her chew.

Later that afternoon, I was sitting on the steps outside my room, staring at a yoga book. Eventually, Whitney appeared, climbing the stairs to her room across from mine. I pretended to read, waiting for her to pass, but she sat down in front of me.

"So you should probably eat more, or you're going to pass out. And if you pass out, you might have to be airlifted out of here, and that would be expensive."

A nervous smile spread across my face. "But I don't feel like eating. I'm not hungry."

"Well, I got news for you. People need to eat to live."

I looked into her light blue eyes and then at the dark curly hair brushing against her shoulders. Her face was so close to mine. I lowered my gaze, watching her chest rise and fall with each breath. She put her hand on my shoulder.

"Look, I know I'm not the greatest example," she said, "but I'm certainly not being as extreme as you are right now. Please eat. I'm serious."

"Okay," I said, unable to shed my nervous smile.

"Okay?" she said, smiling back, hand on my shoulder, moment suspended, lingering, sun in my eyes, midday heat, gentle wind rippling the clothes hanging over the line at the bottom of the stairs. "Okay, then," she said, releasing my shoulder and turning to go into her room. I stared at her hair until it disappeared behind the door. It was the same thing I'd done at age fourteen: starving myself until someone noticed what I was doing and told me to eat, as simple as that. Whitney was so in tune with me, she did it so quickly. I shook my head. I was too self-aware at this point in my life to be behaving this way, such a backward leap. But there was still that antagonistic voice in my head: *You worthless little bitch, you are weak for giving in so easily.* What was this voice? It couldn't have been me. But it existed inside me; if it wasn't me, who was it? *Fuck you, voice, I'm feeding myself whether you like it or not.*

I went to the ashram shop to buy dried apricots, figs, almonds, and cashews. I sat back down on the stairs by my room and consumed everything as fast as I could. Crunching and gnawing, I barely tasted anything, wanting to just give my stomach something to digest. *I'm sorry, body. You don't deserve to be treated this way.*

Nerves surged through my stomach and chest every time Whitney was near me after that conversation. She could see straight through me, such a fierce reflecting pool. I felt a convergence of lust, sisterly love, and fear toward her all at once.

That night at dinner, I sat next to Elisa and force-fed myself a normal-sized meal despite my protesting stomach and head. At one point, I accidentally bumped Elisa's elbow and whispered, "Sorry." She didn't flinch, look up from her plate, or acknowledge me in any way. I thought it strange and watched her through the rest of the meal. She had filled her plate with mountainous portions and was shoveling the food in very quickly, keeping her head down, seeming to be somewhere far removed, deep inside herself. She continued to sit there like that after everyone else's plates had been cleared. I scooted closer to her. Her jaw was clenched and her shoulders tight up by her ears. Her back ballooned up with breath and deflated just as quickly. Then it happened again with increased speed. She was hyperventilating, her elbows on the table, head supported by her hands. Tears ran down her arms.

I reached my left hand under her arm and placed my palm on her sternum, then began to rub in slow circular motions. She did not reject the contact, but rather cried more, sobbing sounds escaping from her mouth, her back heaving harder. As I continued to rub her sternum, the hyperventilation and tears gradually subsided. She straightened her hunched back, brought her hands to the table, and closed her eyes, her face streaked with tear residue. Keeping my hand moving in slow circles against her sternum, I stood up and moved behind her, placing my right hand over my left, maintaining slow, gentle circles with an ounce more pressure. She breathed into my hands.

Night had descended. I listened to the mingling of crickets with the low buzzing of the fluorescent overhead lights, let my eyes close, and began to scan through my own body. The pain in my stomach and head was dull and hardly noticeable. Every time I took the focus off myself, I felt infinitely better. That's why I was drawn to healing work. I had to remember that.

I gradually slowed the circles until I stopped them completely and let my hands rest against Elisa's sternum. She took a deep breath. I lifted my right hand off my left and rested it on the center of her back, so her front and back were equally supported. She took an even deeper breath. I peeled my hands off her body slowly enough to leave a lingering sensation. After a moment, she turned to look up at me and grabbed my hand.

"Thank you," she said.

"Of course," I said, and smiled.

We walked back to our room together. Halfway there, she hooked elbows with mine. She never told me what triggered her panic attack, and I never asked. It didn't matter; I understood panic attacks and was able to give her the exact thing I always wanted when I was in the midst of one. By the time we returned to our room, our roommates were asleep. We brushed our teeth, then kissed each other's cheeks.

"Good night, sweet dreams," I said.

"Thank you again, lovie," she said. From then on, she always called me "Lovie."

Just when I thought my stomach problems were finally clearing up and my energy was returning, on the morning of our third day off, I woke with a disarming amount of fatigue. My body weight felt tremendous, and I was absolutely sick to my stomach. I writhed angrily around in my bed, my thoughts closing in on me. I tried to meditate, unsuccessfully. I was working myself up to the point of panic. Maybe I was being attacked by some strange Indian parasite. Maybe I would never get better. Maybe I had an incurable third world disease that was going to kill me.

I couldn't take it anymore. I hoisted myself out of bed and into the bathroom, where I managed to fill a plastic bucket with hot water and pour it slowly over my naked body. The heat made me tingle all over. Afterward, I lay out on the concrete in the sun as my generous massage therapist neighbor, Samantha, pressed her fingertips methodically point by point along my tense shoulders, neck, and skull. The pressure in my temples lifted slightly, and I was able to sleep through most of the morning while everyone went off to the city. But when I woke to the silence and the stillness in the afternoon, all by myself, I again felt panicked. My heart was racing, I was sweating, I felt trapped in my bed, in my skin, in my sick stomach, pounding skull, desperate. I tried to breathe myself back to calm but was struggling immensely. As I lay there, the hours crawled by, and eventually my roommates came back. They were telling me all about their day in the city when suddenly I felt my head absolutely start to spin, my heart sped up, and I got scared I was going to actually have a heart attack.

"Guys, something seriously fucked up is happening in my body right now. I don't know what's wrong. I don't know what to do. Fuck!" I screamed.

"Let's go find Kate," said Elisa. As she pulled me by the arm, I passed Whitney on the way and felt the familiar electricity course through me.

"What's going on with you?" Whitney asked, turning to walk with me.

"I just... I fucking... I don't know... I..." I trailed off.

We ran into Kate at the bottom of the hill.

"What's wrong?" she asked.

"I feel like my heart is squeezing in my chest. I can't breathe," I said, tears running down my face, my hand pressed against my sternum. She gave me lavender and homeopathic stress relief and sleeping pills, Tylenol, and an antibiotic. I thanked her and continued to cry while Whitney sat beside me and Elisa rubbed my back. I closed my eyes and focused on the palm of her hand moving slowly and rhythmically up and down my back. Gradually, my body became still and calm. In that moment, I loved Elisa more than I had ever loved anyone. She continued to rub the middle of my back in slow circles. The warmth of her hand radiated through my torso. My closed eyes pointed to the space between my eyebrows, moving deeper into the blackness. I began to listen, past the crickets and the wind. I felt the palm of Elisa's hand moving against my back, but Elisa the human fell away. The ashram fell away. India fell away. The world fell away. My life fell away. I lost myself. I was not me. I was nothing. No thing. No body.

When I finally opened my eyes, the first thing I saw was Whitney's face.

"Okay, so you need to make a decision that tomorrow you are better," she said. "Decide that tomorrow is going to be a great day. I'm all for taking care of yourself and doing what you need to do. You feel sick, okay. A little mental disruption for a couple of days is fine. But now you have to snap yourself out of it before you can't."

"Okay, you're right. Tomorrow is going to be a great day."

Her spot-on words made me snap back. This was a matter of mind control. My wiser mind had to lasso its sour half and steer it back to a positive course. Determined to get back on track, I went to the ashram shop after dinner to peruse the books. I trailed my fingers along the paperback spines, absorbing such titles as *Yoga and Psychology*, *The Ancient Tantric Techniques of Yoga and Kriya*, and *Yoga for*

Women, pausing when I reached the title, *Sure Ways to Self-Realization.* Sure ways, huh? Was there a money-back guarantee? Testimonials? I let out a sigh. If only I could realize myself. Realize what already was. This self that already was. What was there to realize? I left the shop and walked slowly through the night air back to my room, staring at the masses of flying beetles hovering around lamplights on my way. *It's time to make a decision. Tomorrow you are better.*

Gratitude

With only a week left of the training, I made up my mind to lunge forward with great energy and get as much out of everything as possible. At first my determined mind wrestled vehemently with its own negative toddler-like protests, still wanting to be able to cry and be sick. But my negative brain was weakened by the weight of determination. With each micro lesson I taught, I grew more relaxed. Teaching was becoming its own form of meditation, requiring my full presence to guide students from pose to pose. I found that having to embody the calm positive energy necessary to teach yoga was even more transcendent than being a student; I had to get myself there of my own volition and realized, with proper concentration, I really was capable of harnessing this state at will.

From the beginning of the course, we were continually reminded that yoga went beyond the physical poses, that it was a complete science of life. Patanjali, author of the *Yoga Sutras*, discussed yoga as an eight-limbed practical guide to harmonizing the mind, body, and spirit, ultimately leading to enlightenment. The eight limbs are as follows: *yamas* (social disciplines), *niyamas* (individual disciplines), *asanas* (body postures), *pranayama* (breathing exercises), *pratyahara* (withdrawal of the senses), *dharana* (concentration), *dhyana* (meditation), and *samadhi* (enlightenment). The further into the course, the more fully I absorbed the concepts of the complete practice.

Everything in life is impermanent and uncertain. I could be racked with perpetual anxiety over this, generating constant suffering for myself, or I could make a different choice. I came to see enlightenment as giving oneself fully to the moment while simultaneously embracing uncertainty and impermanence. Practicing yoga was the way to get there. The more I practiced and taught, the stronger this understanding of enlightenment resonated. Of course, I couldn't completely rid myself of anxious moments. They still barreled in with every stressful thought. But I was getting better at feeling these moments, acknowledging their reality, and letting them pass without allowing them to consume me. While I still had a long way to go, I felt myself becoming increasingly self-aware, moving closer to balance.

While listening to the lecture on the criteria for passing our final teaching lesson, I scribbled some words on a piece of notebook paper. Then I folded it seven equal times, took the wad of chewed gum out of my mouth, and stuck the paper under the desk, thinking maybe someone would find it someday, some other twenty-six-year-old Jewish girl with brown hair and blue eyes who had traveled halfway around the world to study the ancient secrets of extraordinary living. She'd be sitting in the same lecture, preparing to teach her final lesson before becoming a certified yoga teacher, and her right knee would bump against the folded paper. "What is this?" she'd think, and yank the paper off the bottom of the desk. She'd unfold it seven times until she found: *October 10, 2009. Still looking.*

The night before teaching my final lesson, I found a great meditation spot after dinner. It was outside, on the edge of a concrete bench on the grass. For several minutes, I sat cross-legged and looked up at the stars, all of them so bright and piercing. I placed my palms over my knees, closed my eyes, and focused on the surrounding sensations. I heard crickets chirping, voices chattering in the distance. A cool, light breeze grazed my skin.

I thought about the Jewish summer camp I'd attended as a child, memories that the ashram experience naturally triggered. It was a similar setup: beautiful surroundings, living in a close-knit community, spending all day every day together, all that spiritual energy. For the first time in several years, I really missed camp. I opened my eyes, looked at the stars, and mourned camp's passage. I started singing Hebrew prayers and songs from camp and cried.

My thoughts flowed to my father; unbelievable how much time had passed. I missed him so much. I thought about my mother; my heart pained with gratitude. I thanked her for all her selfless efforts, unconditional love and support. I closed my eyes again, losing myself in the cacophony of sounds, but not attaching to any of them: crickets, voices, rustling leaves, slight breeze. Breathing in and out, so effortless. After all the Sanskrit chanting to Lord Shiva, Brahma, Vishnu, Devo, I was sitting in the middle of the ashram singing Hebrew prayers with every part of me, praying for patience, compassion for myself and others, confidence, courage, love, and faith. I thanked myself for all the hard work I had done, for all the achievements and growth. I thanked myself for coming to India.

The next morning, I taught a full one-hour yoga class: my final lesson. At the end of the class, I sat with my eyes closed, spine erect, my hands face up on my knees. As I led the group in chanting eleven *oms*, the sound vibrated through my cheeks, throat, and chest, and I felt elated and hopeful. My heart was full, nearly to the point of bursting. It was a feeling I welcomed. I always wanted to live at that level.

At our closing ceremony, we all sat in the main hall in a half circle while Vishwas Mandlik, founder of the ashram, stood before us in his orange robe. A giant wooden *Om* symbol hung on the wall behind him. He lit a candle then turned to speak to us.

"You should all be proud of yourselves," he said, panning his gaze across the twenty faces before him. "Today, you will all receive yoga teacher certificates. But if you don't teach, the certificate means nothing. So please, teach. There is so much stress and suffering in society; you are needed. Always remember that. Now, if anyone would like to come up here and say a few words before I hand out the certificates…"

He stepped to the side. Elisa got up first. She was crying, her eyes pink behind her black-rimmed glasses and her body shaking. "Before this program, my life really was shit. I was scared to come here, and I never thought I really had what it took to teach yoga, but yesterday I taught a whole class and it went so well; I can't believe it…thank you." As she walked back to her seat, she removed her glasses to wipe her eyes. I looked around the room to see other people's eyes filling with tears.

Another girl, Hillary, got up and said, "We are all adventurers and should really pat ourselves on the back for taking this risk. We didn't know what we were in for, but we came anyway because we are all looking for something deeper in our lives. I never keep in touch with anybody, but I would really love to keep in touch with you, find out how your teaching is going. It would be great to share with each other, you know, give each other some tips. Thanks, guys, for a really amazing experience."

Then compulsion seized me, and I stood and walked to the front. I took a look at everyone, inhaled, and said, "I really can't stop thinking about what Gandhar said about yoga and fear, how yoga brings you in touch with the fact that if you're lucky, you get ninety to one hundred years in this life, and with this realization, you lose all sense of fear. That never quite sank in for me until that moment." I paused, swallowed, and said, "I really want to live an extraordinary life." I sat down quickly as adrenaline coursed through my body.

There was a long silence before Vishwas stood back up and Kate went to join him. "We will now call you up one at a time and present you with your certificate," she said. During the procession, I thought about how we would soon be parting from each other and, despite Hillary's suggestion that we all keep in touch, I knew once everyone got involved with their home lives, the likelihood of that was slim. We lived all over the world; most of us would probably never speak with or see each other again. I thought about Celia, my best friend from camp. We hadn't spoken in ten years, and I still missed her.

Some people left immediately after the ceremony. Others, myself included, stayed a couple of extra nights. Elisa would be leaving the next night, so we decided to spend the day together, starting with a morning walk to the nearby town of Trimbak. When we got there, we sat down at a dirty table surrounded by flies, and I sipped the most delicious chai I'd ever tasted. Then we wandered through the streets, bought some sweets and necklaces, and took pictures until we found ourselves at the edge of town by a temple facing a wide green field at the base of an overlapping cluster of giant hills. Women in saris and men dressed all in white stood in line to enter the temple as a bell sounded. All were barefoot. The sun shone brightly on their faces. I rolled up my short sleeves, closed my eyes, and tilted my head back, exposing my shoulders and throat to the sky.

We walked past the temple, further into the green, then found a spot in the middle of the field where we sat down cross-legged, closed our eyes, and listened. There were no people around. Every-thing was still. Distant chants echoed through the hills. We opened our eyes and saw a line of goats traipse across the field. We looked at each other, not speaking, continuing to listen. A potent energy filled the space and flooded us both. We felt blissful, wanting so much to hold onto the moment but knowing, like all things, it would soon pass. Elisa and I had promised each other we'd keep in touch, talked of traveling to Thailand together the following sum-mer. Twenty percent of me believed it, eighty percent knew this was the end for us. We were in each other's lives for a brief win-dow; I loved her, and I would never forget her.

The following day, Whitney, Samantha, and I shared a taxi to the Nasik train station for the four-hour train ride to Mumbai. Samantha would be leaving us in Mumbai, and Whitney and I would be spending one night together in a hotel; we both had flights out the next evening. As the taxi drove us away from the ashram, we saw a woman on the side of the road transporting a giant mound of cow dung in her bare hands and smiling. "Just carrying the morning shit," Samantha quipped. It was a perfect final lesson for leaving the ashram: Smile even while you're carrying a bunch of shit because hey, it's a beautiful morning. Together, we chanted the Sanskrit mantra with which we'd closed all our yoga sessions, now the closing prayer of our ashram experience.

Once on the train, I stared out the window for a bit, watching the city blur past and turn to vast expanses of green as my thoughts began to swirl. There was so much feeling spiraling inside me that it might actually burst through my chest and fly over the mountains. I hoped I could maintain all I had learned once I was back on my own. I thought about these beautiful human connections in just one month's time. My gaze trailed thatch-roofed huts, women draped in bright saris, sliding against their dirty legs, as they walked along the road with baskets on their heads. I tried to cement these sights in my memory, knowing that this could potentially be the last of India I would ever see.

I looked across from me at Whitney, her head resting against the window, eyes closed. I replayed our conversations. God, I loved her. *Do you need me to rub your back? What do you need? Tell me and I'll do it. How can I serve you?*

I returned my gaze to the window and remembered the lady in Varanasi covered in dirt with her sleeping baby in her arms. I would never be able to erase that image. "Please, ma'am," she had said, desperately grabbing my shirt, "I'm hungry."

I'm sorry, I can't. I'm sorry, I can't. I'm sorry I, I'm sorry I. Sorry I, sorry, sorry, sorry—

I opened my journal and began to scribble furiously:

Let's all hold hands lying in corpse pose in a field as a cobra crawls over our necks, eyes closed, chanting "Om" with the appropriate counts: A-2, U-3, M-8. The voice of the yoga teacher should be calm and soothing. The aim of yoga is to gain mastery over the mind, to be freed from oneself.

Samantha was sitting beside me. I looked over at her, her eyes also closed, headphones in her ears. First she would go, then it would just be Whitney and me, and then just me, heading back alone to New York City, with its hot showers, soft mattresses, clean linens, and proper washing machines. And so? What an opportunity. I was alive. I had so much moving and breathing to do. Torrents of freshly oxygenated blood circulated through my limbs and warmed me.

I looked back down at my journal and scribbled away:

Life, I love you. From now on, I will work with love.

I closed the journal, found my headphones, and put them in my ears, turning on Bob Dylan's "Lily, Rosemary and the Jack of Hearts." *Okay*, I thought, *time to close my eyes. Now I'll rest, kick back and believe. And above all, I promise I won't be afraid.*

In the taxi from the airport back to my Brooklyn apartment, the sun was setting. A hot pink glow hovered around the old brick buildings, and my insides shook with possibility. My roommate was not home when I arrived, so I dumped my bags in my room and darted out the door to climb the ladder to the roof. I hoisted myself up, planted my feet, looked at the sky, and made out the few stars that had not been swallowed up by the city lights. I opened my arms, letting the cool November breeze hit me like falling leaves. It was cold; my lower extremities were raw and exposed. But I just breathed in the chill. The deeper the breath, the more my blood warmed it. My heart pumped harder and faster, lungs expanding and contracting, body doing what it does every day to keep me alive. Being. Existing. Boundless gratitude, so much so, there was pain. *Why do all extremes become pain?* I closed my eyes and opened them, closed them and opened them, radiating, welcoming the exchange of gases in the form of air and light. My arms stretched like a rubber band, heart wide open, swallowing the moonlight.

Tears fell down my cheeks, reflecting light like diamonds, jeweled puddles on my chest. I caught the water in my hands, threw it back up, and offered it to the sky. The moon was relentless. She was not going anywhere, at least not until morning. I looked up at her, took a bath in her light, then fell down on my knees, flipped onto my back, extended my legs, and looked up. A plane crossed the sky, just like the plane that had flown me across the Atlantic Ocean from the other side of the world. What a technological miracle. I exploded with deeper tear-filled convulsions, bathing in tears and moonlight under the stars. *Where was I then, where am I now? Who was I then, who am I now? What is this body that I live in? What is this form? What is all this feeling? This intense desire to create something beautiful—why is beauty so painful?*

Thanksgiving was on its way, as was the day after Thanksgiving, which would make it nine years since my father died. I stood up, lifted my arms, spread my fingers wide, and missed him with all of my being. I got down on my knees and let my head drop to the ground. I knew he would be proud. I wept for myself, for my life, for my experience, for all that had happened and all that had yet to be.

****

My face is pressed against the yoga mat. My arms are extended long in front of me. My knees are bent under my chest, hips on my heels. I am in child's pose, breathing deeply in and out. I curl my toes under and extend my hips high to the ceiling for downward dog. I bend one leg, then the other. Rise up to my toes. Lift my left leg, open my hip. Feel the muscles lengthen off the bone, the tissues expand. My arms are strong. I lower the leg, do the same with my right. Then I jump forward so my feet are between my hands. Half lift my torso. Fall forward. Extend my arms out to the sides all the way up overhead, deep back bend. Heart reaching, chest expanding. Fall forward. One breath, one movement.

As I get further along in the practice, holding the lunges, maintaining the postures, shaking, I have to focus on my breath, which gets deeper and deeper. Chair pose: My hands reach for the ceiling, and I sit back into an imaginary chair. My quads are burning. Sweat pours down my forehead. It's a matter of determination. I will not give up. I will keep breathing. It's all mind. Focus entirely on this moment. This is the only moment.

Acknowledgments

I want to thank Amy Dupcak, Scott Hess, Daniel Foley, Naomi Kriss, and Nicole DeWalt, whose feedback through the writing process has been vital; Sarah-Doe Osborne, Carolyn McCandlish, Julio Pena, Annie Barry, Lorin Taylor, and Shawn Shafner for being comrades in life and art; Sophie Appel for the gorgeous cover and layout; Colleen Toole and Chantal Pavageaux for helping to turn this into a show; Golda Akhgarnia for years of friendship; Tyler Nesler for the love; my siblings Tiffany and Austin, my mom Terry, and finally my dad, David, who encouraged me to write.

Credits

An excerpt from "Mirror, Mirror on the Wall" appeared on Love Your Rebellion, an online site dedicated to body acceptance, feminism and sex positivity.
www.loveyourrebellion.com

"Your Particular Smile" appeared as "One Breath, Then Another" in the print anthology *So Long: Short Memoirs of Loss and Remembrance* by Telling Our Stories Press.
www.tellingourstoriespress.com

"Straight Up to Heaven," an excerpt from "No One Wears Shoes Here," appeared in the print anthology *Runaway Parade: An Anthology: Selected Works By Runaway Parade Artists, Writers and Poets* as well as in Runaway Parade's online publication of art and writing.
www.runawayparade.com

An excerpt from "Silence" appeared in *Underwired Magazine*.
www.underwiredmagazine.com

An excerpt from "Teaching" appeared in Om Times, a holistic green eZine with a spiritual, self-growth perspective for the conscious community.
www.omtimes.com

21042376R00110

Made in the USA
Lexington, KY
03 March 2013